T0130124

This Is NOT My Life!

Coaching the Past to Help Your Future

S.M. Love

authorHOUSE®

AuthorHouse™
1663 Liberty Drive
Bloomington, IN 47403
www.authorhouse.com
Phone: 1 (800) 839-8640

© 2016 S.M. Love. All rights reserved.

No part of this book may be reproduced, stored in a retrieval system, or
transmitted by any means without the written permission of the author.

Published by AuthorHouse 02/17/2016

ISBN: 978-1-5049-7574-2 (sc)
ISBN: 978-1-5049-7555-1 (e)

Library of Congress Control Number: 2016901521

Print information available on the last page.

Any people depicted in stock imagery provided by Thinkstock are models,
and such images are being used for illustrative purposes only.
Certain stock imagery © Thinkstock.

This book is printed on acid-free paper.

Because of the dynamic nature of the Internet, any web addresses or links contained in
this book may have changed since publication and may no longer be valid. The views
expressed in this work are solely those of the author and do not necessarily reflect the
views of the publisher, and the publisher hereby disclaims any responsibility for them.

Acknowledgements

I would like to thank my amazing husband

for his love and inspiration.

We have a choice in our happiness; we just have to choose the right path. My story will show you how easy it is to become lost in someone else's world. It is an example of how what seems like the easy way out is not always so easy in the end.

This book will show you everything I went through in an emotionally abusive relationship. It is meant to shed light on the part we all play in our situations and relationships. I understand how simple it is to turn the other cheek, or just blame someone else for your misfortunes. These writings are to help everyone with a similar story understand the part they play in their own relationships.

Chapter One

Hot sex, fabulous cars, and exotic trips were the snap shots of my relationship in my early twenties. I was still in college and having a rich man was the in thing. I was headed towards a nice career in the hospital, but let's face it in California you dream bigger than the hospital. My goals were a big ring with many flashy things so others could be envious. I was young and had lost track of the fact that a real relationship was about more than material things. I received everything I wanted from Daniel— along with things I did not want. I was in the beginning of a dysfunctional relationship that was surrounded with emotional abuse, covered up by money.

Daniel and I had some really great times, mixed with some questionable times in our new courtship. We were long-term associates, so we assumed it would be a good fit. He was a man I trusted because we had so much in common. We could laugh together for hours, and even lose track of time just talking. I was so wrapped up in our previous friendship from high school, that I didn't analyze our current relationship.

I was 22 years old, and he swept me off my feet like a fairytale. It was hard to see past the extravagant gifts, and luxurious lifestyle he provided for me. For the first 4 months life was "perfect", and argument free. Then out of nowhere we started having trivial disagreements. These spats would end up with him not talking to me for up to two weeks. Most of the other weeks everything would be romantic and argument-free.

It took me a long time to realize how much we were arguing. More often than not, arguments became less because I tiptoed around his triggers. Looking back, I realize now this was a huge warning sign from the

2

beginning of the relationship, but I believed I was in love, so I chose to work it out. I was immature and believed that all adult relationships had these types of problems. I didn't realize that having these issues at the early stage meant down the line it would get worse.

As months passed by and one year changed into the next, we had some really good times; it would be hard to count them all. The 80% good, at this point, definitely outweighed the 20% bad in the relationship. The problem was that he seemed to be just going through the motions, and never really putting his real emotions out there. Don't get me wrong: the presents, and extravagant trips he gave me were amazing. But it always seemed like we were playing roles in a movie until we argued and I cried. It was like he was on autopilot when we were happy, and his real personality came out when we argued. Although the bad with us could be more than bad, after a year of courtship things started to change and become even worse.

I watched the situation change before my eyes, but I never expressed my feelings or position about the relationship. I didn't want our relationship to end because I was afraid to be single. I also was determined to not start over with someone else. We started spending less time together; now he only went out with his friends. If I ever said anything about him going out with his friends, or stated how I didn't like the little bit of time he gave me, I was wrong. If I said one word we were in an argument. These childish mind tricks seemed to keep me at bay for the time being.

If I had been my own life coach then, I would have asked myself a series of questions:

Are you happy with your relationship?

If you are not happy what is keeping you there?

What would help your relationship become more of what you need?

Advice to my past self:

*I would have let myself know that it was okay to be single if a relationship was emotionally abusive. Emotional abuse is never okay, and would only get worse with time. It might be better to stay friends versus a romantic relationship.

*Remember, you do not have to deal with any type of abuse in life. I do understand it can take a little while before most people recognize emotional abuse (verbal abuse, mind control).

Since I wasn't a life coach at this time, I stayed through all of the hard patches. I was loyal to a fault. To my surprise, he still managed to ask me to move away with him to his home on the East Coast a year into the relationship. Moving meant I had to drop my whole life, including my job, to revolve around his needs, and it was a scary thought. But, like many others, I had love blinders on and made the move.

I had a man and I wanted to keep him so I did what it took. I wasn't thinking about how my life would be affected. I was just living in the moment, and enjoying the ride. I didn't think about how he would now be in total control because he would be supporting me. My parents said that with his personality type it would be a mistake, but I still avoided all the warning signs. I swore that moving would show my love and trust to make us closer.

Unfortunately, these are thoughts many woman have when they just want to be in love. Not necessarily in love with the person they are with, but just loved by someone.

I arrived on the East Coast three weeks earlier than we had both intended. A family member of mine had just passed away so I was going to attend the funeral. It was warm and humid back east with light rains, very different from the sunny days and beach I had left behind. I was just so excited to live together because it was a new adventure neither of us had ever experienced. I was so overwhelmed with things going on I could have never guessed what was going to happen next.

I had been in town three days and Daniel took me everywhere: movies, fancy dinner, clubs, and even the theater for a play. By the time the weekend ended we had been living together for four days, and it was time for him to return to work.

He awoke and went to work early Monday, and shortly after I woke up and started making myself at home. I started unpacking and cleaning to some soul tunes on the music channel. I was being a "good girlfriend", cleaning the townhouse from top to bottom. About an hour and a half in, my heart would be shattered into pieces I could not mend. A year and four months was flushed down the toilet.

After cleaning his bathroom and the living room area I worked my way over to the third bedroom. I was almost done cleaning when I found a video camera under one of the pillows as I was straightening the bed. The LED part of the camera was still popped open, so I wanted to see what someone had been watching or recording. Being nosey, I pressed play and saw three people having wild sex in the room I was trying to clean—and one of the participants was Daniel.

My heart must have skipped two beats at that moment. Anger, sadness, stupidity, and hurt all set in at once. Then my heart began to beat out of my chest. I pressed "pause" to try to think things through before reacting. While tossing thoughts back and forth, a light bulb popped on: this could have totally been an old video. Maybe he was just watching the good old single days before having a live-in girlfriend. That had to be it! Maybe he was just freaking out about having a live-in girlfriend; I couldn't be mad at anything that happened before me.

Questions I should have asked myself:

Do you want to be with someone that is watching his past sex acts?

Are you really okay now that you know about this type of behavior?

Advice to my past self:

*Disrespect comes in all forms and this was not very healthy. You have to take a stand on what you will not deal with from anyone.

* *Remember, when you take a stand people will respect you more in the long run.*

Like anyone else these questions never entered my mind, not even once. My thoughts just raced back and forth until the CSI agent in me came out. Then I thought about rewinding the tape to the beginning. I wanted to see if my loving boyfriend had his brand-new tattoo in the video. If so, I would have cold hard evidence that he was cheating on me. I hit rewind and play. A minute and a half into the video, I saw his tattoo and hit pause. There he was, cheating on me with not one, but two women at once. Why the hell would he even ask me to move in if this is what he wanted?

To add insult to injury, the girls who were with him had all the qualities he said he didn't want. Great! At first the only thought I had was, why do men always cheat with people they say they don't like? This always seemed to baffle me, even with stories I heard from friends.

The commentary on this tape was so vulgar, and he seemed very happy and content. It was so outrageous. Was this one of his natural habits?

I was now sick to my stomach, and for good reason. I did not understand this type of behavior.

The first thought that popped into my head was to go to his office, make a scene, and slap him! This was a normal irrational reaction in the moment, and it quickly faded. Pacing back and forth, I called my best friend and told her some of what happened, screaming and crying. She tried to help me rationalize my thoughts. She also helped me look for a ticket to fly home. After an hour of venting, I started packing my clothes. I turned on my soulful slow jams to help calm my nerves.

About three hours later, I was now very calm. In the center of my tornado everything was peaceful, with chaos all around. I went back in the room and grabbed the video camera to hook it up to the big screen television in his living room. Then I took the liberty of pausing it right when he was showing off his muscles, and having the most fun. When his truck pulled up I started playing the video and sat by the front door.

This was definitely a defining moment in our relationship. All of the images were burned into my memory. When he walked in and saw the video he automatically tried to lie. But since I had played detective for eight hours, I let him know that I knew this was a recent video. **Why lie when you're caught?**

He fell into immediate regret and fake tears. It was all a great act that I could barely handle. Daniel was only sad and sorry because he was caught. I continued to ask questions, and he continued to lie to my face. He thought I was stupid enough to believe him.

I boldly asked a simple question, "How many times have you cheated on me?" He said, "That was it! I swear to God!" I am very surprised lightning did not strike at this moment. Then I stopped asking questions and said, "Just tell me it has been more than you can count." But this man was so into his lie that he stuck to his guns. He said what I saw on the video was the only time he cheated.

After throwing things and yelling, I gave in and went to a silent dinner with this cheater. I was between a rock and a hard place. I had just given up my good job to be with him. I didn't want to go home immediately because my father would be right. Plus I had some money, but I didn't want to spend my last bit leaving him. In the back of my mind I knew I did not want to leave him permanently. So using my last bit of money to make a big scene would have been a waste. Once we returned to his home, I refused to sleep in any room there. So I laid on the couch with all of my bags still packed.

Questions I should have asked myself:

Do you still want to be with him?

Do you want to work it out with someone who could easily lie to your face?

How much longer are you going to put up with the way he treats you?

Do you really believe that this relationship is better than being single?

Advice to my past self:

Leave and get out of the relationship. Start fresh, and let my parents know what was going on.

Remember, to always confide in people who care about you. Your parents don't want to see you hurt, and can provide good advice. It is not a good thing to hide from those who love you. Also, I would have told myself to stop doing wife like things, when I was only a girlfriend.

I tried to mentally heal the next day, because he begged me not to leave before he returned home from work. My thoughts were all over the place. I tried to continue cleaning to ease my mind. I know it seems weird, but it helped me to relax. This of course would prove to be another challenging day. I didn't understand why I wasn't on a plane to go home. I was trying to just make myself feel better by talking to my best friend, while I cleaned up his bedroom.

I was honestly trying to just make myself comfortable at my boyfriend's home. I was still hurt and disappointed about his actions, but I loved him. He seemed like he was going to make sure that everything was going to be okay, so I was trying to sweep my feelings under the rug. I wanted this relationship to work because I had put so much effort into it. I was trying to convince myself that he wouldn't betray me again.

Before I could even get some clear concise thoughts talked out, my heart felt another flutter. I was staring at a videotape on the floor of the bedroom that was marked "xxx." While staring at the tape, I got instantly upset. Then I told my best friend I would call her later. As I shook my head I put the tape into the VCR. My heart already knew what I would find. This time Daniel really had made his own little chopped up porno. My thoughts raced back and forth.

This was not the man I thought I knew growing up. I knew him for so long that I couldn't believe what my eyes were seeing. This all seemed so far off character. He was a professional man this could not be who he really was in private.

I was in denial, but I was no longer shocked by these actions. The woman who was performing a number on my boyfriend happened to be wearing the same necklace he had made for me, or so I thought.

Every girl got the same jewelry?

Was all of this really happening?

After all of the sexual acts he sat and gave commentary about them, and this just perplexed me. My thoughts were very unclear, but one good question popped up: Why don't you just leave this situation right away, and never speak to him again?

Questions I should have asked myself:

What makes you believe someone should treat you this way?

Are you just fearful of being alone?

Advice to my past self:

*You need to leave. Being single is nothing to be afraid of you will eventually find someone who wants to be with only you.

Remember, someone who will cheat on you with multiple people will usually keep cheating.

This time I refused to wait eight hours to confront him this time, so I contacted him at work. He was in the middle of a meeting, but came running home. Once he got there he was so nervous and had no answers. He just kept telling me he was sorry. Still, pathetically, I stayed even with all the lies because I thought I had nowhere to go. I was making myself a victim subconsciously. I was scared to be alone, and convinced that he was right: I might not find a better man.

Whenever we argued he always let me know that he was the best guy I would ever have. These words always played in the back of my mind. I knew better, but for some reason I could not get myself to move on.

He suggested we buy a home together and move in quickly. Ignoring all of the thoughts in the back of my mind, yet again, I agreed.

I have no idea why I did not think things through, but I let the relationship move forward. Although the search to find a beautiful home went smoothly, and was even fun at times, I was so unhappy. We bought new furniture that I picked out, and we did all the things I wanted. But the images of him with all those women were burned into my brain. They would come up out of the blue, and I knew I had to leave him. Three weeks after moving into our new home, while he was away for work, my self-questioning became more intense. All of the thoughts I had settled in!

I didn't want to be with someone who watched himself cheating on me. It would be impossible to trust this man, and who knows how much more he had actually done or was doing. I was unsure of how to leave our relationship, but I definitely needed to get away from him.

On a dark day, after an idiotic fight I had with Daniel, I packed all my things and left the house. He was gone for work again, so it would be my easy break from this madness. I knew when he got home he would lose it, so I left my version of a Dear John letter. About six hours after I left, he started calling and texting me. He even started calling some of my good friends. After about the eighth call from my best friend I answered to let her know I was safe. She asked me what happened, and where I was staying. I reassured her that I was okay without much detail, and let her know to pick me up at the airport the next day.

Meanwhile, my phone kept beeping because Daniel would not stop calling.

Daniel was trying to find me, but nobody knew where I was because I had family come and get me. The only person I had shared any "real information" with was a Pastor. Nobody needed to know all of the horrible details, and I was keeping it that way. I then finally answered the phone when he called.

The questions came one after another, with barely a breath in between. "Where are you? Why did you leave? How did you leave?" And his infamous line, "Please don't do this!" As we talked I could feel the lies through the cell phone. My stomach was in knots from just thinking about everything that had happened. I had tuned him out so I got off the phone as nicely as possible.

The next morning I went to the airport and caught the earliest flight possible, to my place 3,000 miles away. By the next afternoon, Daniel was calling and begging to pick me up so we could work it out. When I told him

I was all the way back home he flipped out. This was unknown territory for him, and he didn't like it.

Nobody had ever left Daniel, and he always got what he wanted when he wanted it. The fact that I left was not okay with him. Daniel now tried to turn things around on me. He began to question my love for him, and asked if I really even cared.

I was over being manipulated, or so I thought. I let him know that I would rather show him real love. I wanted him to know that lies and disrespect were not love. I was not staying around to let him lie to me, and disrespect me. It was not going to happen. As days passed, I talked to my Pastor to help with my faith, but I started to miss Daniel. Whenever I had weak moments and wanted to call him, I would watch one of those nasty tapes he made. I had packed the tapes with my things so he wouldn't have them when I left. I thought taking them to possibly burn them would help me forget the acts committed.

Questions I should have asked myself:

What makes you want to torture yourself?

What makes you want to relive something that hurt you?

Is this really aiding you in moving forward?

Do you believe this type of behavior is healthy?

Advice to my past self:

*You are in a really unhealthy relationship, and you should start taking better care of yourself. This type of behavior will most likely get worse.

Remember: Unhealthy is unhealthy and it requires help. Professional help from a therapist.

Chapter Two

Just as I thought my feelings were in check and I could face the facts that we were over, Daniel came chasing after me. He showed up at my home unexpectedly four days after I left, and I didn't know what I should do. I started to question myself, like I always did when it came to Daniel.

I was starting to believe that he was actually being sincere when he said he was sorry. (Here I was being tricked yet again.) Daniel had flown 3000 miles to win me back, and was missing important meetings. I didn't know what else to think, outside believing him. He gave me money, and told me to take my time to come back to our home. I was so confused, but I was in love with him so I just said, "okay."

When he left my apartment I called my Pastor for counseling. None of his advice seemed helpful, because I was not being very receptive. He told me to pray and God would give me the answers that I needed. Instead of attempting to hear what God had to say, I went back east three days later.

All seemed "well." The trust we had was broken, but I chose to focus on other things. We were back to our normal routine, and time moved fast. Three months later Daniel got down on one knee to ask me to be his wife. We were in front of multiple family members, I was cornered, but of course I said, "Yes."

I had truly mixed emotions about the whole situation. It was a feeling no woman ever imagines having when it comes to a proposal. Why was he even doing this? We were not where we should be as a couple. All I could do at the moment was cry at the loving gesture. But I don't know if I was crying because I was happy, or because I was confused.

Questions I should have asked myself:

Would you marry someone you can't trust?

What are your core values for marriage?

Would you violate your values to be with someone you question?

What is making you not listening to your feelings?

Advice to my past self:

*Listen to your feelings: they will always tell you the right thing to do. Your feelings will help you guard your heart from hurt, but you have to be in a sound mind to listen.

Remember: Always hold tight to your values. Don't let go of your core values for others.

Weeks passed, and at night time I always asked Daniel the same question: was he sure about getting married. He said he was, but I was still not convinced it was right. Trying to make him happy had become my specialty, so we kept going with the wedding plans. We picked a date, colors, and even agreed on a place. The truth was I could feel this was a downward spiral, and the beginning of the end. I should have ended the relationship, but I was so emotionally involved. I was now truly fearful of being single, and I was too loyal to a fault.

Even though I knew we were way overdue to break up, I just hid my feelings of unhappiness. It was so hard to be with someone whose every move I questioned. My only release was writing, and going to dance class so I wouldn't go crazy. It was hard to pretend at work functions, appearances, and dinners to be the model couple. Our relationship was completely opposite of what others saw in public.

We went to premarital counseling two nights a week, and I didn't know why we were pushing forward. He never wanted to do the "at home" activities, and after a couple of weeks we stopped going. He didn't like the fact that the pastor told us to practice abstinence before getting married. He said it would help our appreciation for one another. Daniel was not enthused about him mentioning anything to do with our sex life.

I should have known it was over when he told me that if we stopped having sex he would just find someone else who would until we married. This was a huge red flag waving in my face, but I ignored it.

He said nasty things with ease all of the time. I could see what he was doing with my mind, but somehow my heart fell for the tricks. He constantly let me know that I couldn't find better. He would then turn around and buy me fancy gifts. Life was so confusing on a daily basis. This was no way to live before a marriage. Unwillingly, I started to become a doormat, smiling and taking the nonsense. Knowing I deserved more, I kept accepting the bare minimum out of my relationship.

Questions I should have asked myself:

What would make you stand up for what you believe in?

What do you really need in a relationship?

What do you want in a spouse?

How happy are you with your relationship in this present moment?

Advice to my past self:

*You should always put your own happiness first. If you are not happy, nobody else around you can make you happy. You need to leave to save the self-esteem you have left.

Remember: Your self-esteem is your responsibility, and you should not let anybody take a toll on it.

I noticed, during the engagement, that we started drifting further from one another. We both focused on things that had nothing to do with our relationship, even though this was a perfect time to focus on it. Still, we eagerly made plans for our wedding, he was always more excited than me. I was now living in a trance, doing everything I was supposed to do for show, but dying on the inside.

He made me feel like I was secondary, and yet very important at the same time. This was something he did so well. I was never a person who experienced mixed emotions before I met him. Now, I was just sitting around, waiting for drama, and creating drama. I was aiding and abetting a cheater in silence. I was faking being in love, knowing that love had been gone for a long time. But we kept taking trips and passing time. Before we knew it he was back to the busy season at work.

This time when I was back in our east coast home, I did more for me. I was just trying to keep myself happy. I attended dance school, landed movie roles, and hit salsa clubs on my own. I even made new friends to hang out with and keep my mind off my home life. I was happy with myself, but not at all in my relationship with my fiancé.

He accused me of cheating because I seemed happy. He couldn't stand to see me happy when it wasn't because of him. I had stopped asking about his every move. All I could think about was why we were getting married when we had so many problems. Yet, I still did nothing.

As Daniel chose to go to strip clubs every weekend, I chose local clubs to go salsa dancing. He always lied about his whereabouts so I stopped asking. I started realizing that my fiancé and I were no longer friends. We were just in a troubled relationship, and I was starting to despise him.

I became so wrapped up in doing my own thing, I forgot about the limitations of a relationship. I didn't tell a guy I befriended that I was engaged. He was a harmless dance partner, and he texted me a little too late one night. That one text message started a nice-sized blow up, like World War III.

Daniel flipped out and called me unimaginable things. It was an innocent text so I knew there was something deep beneath the layers of the conflict. Soon the argument turned violent, and I had no idea where it was going. I was throwing things and breaking furniture, while he was name calling and threating me. He was showing his true colors in front of everyone, as we woke up the whole house with the fighting and yelling. My mother had to stop us from hurting one another, and advised him to leave the house. My friends and parents were present, so were some of his cousins; this was the last thing they needed to witness.

After Daniel left I packed my things and went to a nearby hotel with my parents. I was so ashamed of my reactions to his actions in front of them. I was even angry at myself for close friends seeing this type of interaction between us. I was lucky that I didn't hurt him by throwing things, and that he didn't hit me back. I was now trying to be rational and process everything that happened.

Calling the cops was not an option because I didn't want to embarrass myself, or ruin his career.

When I woke up the next morning all I did was sit in the window of my parents' hotel room. Daniel called and asked where I was, and that he wanted to talk to me in person. I agreed to his wishes as long as we stayed in front of my parents' hotel. I was still shaken from the confrontation. He agreed to my terms, and was at the hotel in less than 15 minutes.

The first thing he did was ask would I ever cheat on him. My answer to his question was no, but I was insulted. He kept talking and it all went silent around me. I had no idea what I was doing anymore. I didn't know why I was in the car with this man. Our relationship was clearly over. He was cheating on me, and I was getting blamed for cheating on him. I was in the worst nightmare, and could not get out.

Questions I should have asked myself:

What is making you stay with someone so mean and hurtful?

How much worse will it get if you stay together?

I attempted to continue listening to him, and then he said something incredibly manipulative. He told me that before this fight, he believed I was a perfect person.

Was this guy serious? Nobody is perfect. I knew now that he felt this could be a way to turn the tables on me if he cheated again. He then had the audacity to say we needed to work on him trusting me. It was all so laughable, and sad at the same time. After being manipulative, he asked me to come home, and I went like a puppy dog to keep the peace. I didn't have time to make a decision because he wanted me home right away. I was no longer thinking for myself. I was just some robot taking orders.

Advice to my past self:

*Run far away from that man. Someone controlling you is never okay for any reason.

Remember: Abuse will get worse as time goes on; you have to take a stand against any negativity as soon as it happens.

Thinking things would be okay, I tried to clean the house that I had torn into shambles. While picking up pieces from mirrors and closets, the interrogation continued. He badgered me day in and day out. This was emotional abuse to the core, but I could not see through it. There was no rest at all from this one incident that he was holding against me. When we returned to the west coast he stayed in his summer home, and I stayed in my own apartment. The apartment was the only thing I had to myself so I kept it. I was still afraid to only live in Daniel's homes. Yet we kept planning our extravagant wedding. The wedding was only three months away, and

I started to feel really funny about it. I started feeling as if he was hiding his true self, and that I was completely lost in the fake world we made up.

The feelings I had were more extreme than my ones prior to the engagement. It felt like he was being more deceiving than usual. I couldn't tell what was going on, but it was something deep.

I was still feeling that our real-world truth was unhappiness. He always denied our unhappiness and said we were okay, so I kept pushing forward. As usual my feelings were on the back burner to what he wanted. I was just trying to keep up all appearances for the outside world, but I felt trapped in my own mind.

We still smiled as one, laughed as one, and the plans were moving along "great." I just wanted us to work for some insane reason. There had been three years invested and I didn't want to flush all that time down the drain.

Than on Sunday morning I woke up around five in the morning. It seemed like God was telling me something. Daniel and I needed to hear the Word and to go to church. When God calls you it is always at the right time, so I just listened. At seven in the morning, I jumped in my car to drive over to Daniel's house so we could go to church.

When I pulled up to the front of his house I got out of the car, and walked up to find the door unlocked. This was very strange because the door was never unlocked, but I proceeded to go upstairs. Once I got upstairs, I opened the bedroom door, and fell immediately into a great state of shock. As I looked around I saw cigarettes on the table, women's clothing everywhere, and someone lying on my side of the bed.

I sat quietly as I thought about what to do. Our wedding was two months away, and things like this were still happening. I could never trust someone like this, ever. Here I was trying to get to early service at church, and here he was playing with another woman. I finally saw what God wanted me to see. Was I going insane? Was this really happening?

I stood over them both so quietly that they didn't even know I was there. I was more than disappointed. In a rage, I started swinging and hitting him. He woke up afraid then tackled me to the ground, screaming my name, and asking how I got in. It showed his true colors. He didn't even care that he was cheating—he cared about how I got in the house. Wow, what was I thinking? Why did I not walk out? He was so toxic to my own sanity.

I chuckled but almost cried because I couldn't believe this situation was happening. We argued back and forth for about five minutes. Then I asked the other woman how long they had been together. Her classic answer was, "I don't know, ask him." I could see she was just another woman trying to "get in in where she fit in." She was in it for his money, because she didn't say another word, or get dressed. He was very wealthy and women always flocked to him. But this wasn't about her; this was about him. We left her sitting in the house as we went to his parents' house to finish arguing.

He was never the type to handle our problems on his own; his mother was always somehow involved. The first excuse out of his mouth, at his mom's house, was that he believed I was cheating on him. Of course this would be his first defense: to turn the situation around on me. I went over the horror story as I took my ring off and threw it at him. I let him know that he could go back to his "other girl" in the bed. His mother then yelled at him and let him know he was ruining things. She told him he needed to make things right.

Things were never going to be right in this relationship again, and I knew it in my heart. His father drove him back to his home, and I sat at his parents' house for hours in dismay before I finally got the strength to drive home. The drive seemed so long and confusing because I was so embarrassed by my situation.

I knew somehow his friends were now involved, and possibly even his mother. She was to calm during the situation, and didn't seem shocked at all. Everyone was lying to me. The deceit was so deep I didn't want to know.

I just didn't know what part everyone was playing in the lie. I let my best friend know that night the wedding was off, and I was going to tell everyone else in the morning.

The next morning, I woke up and started calling some of my close friends to tell them the news. Before I could get to my third phone call, Daniel's mother called me. She asked if I was okay, and then she asked if I could please speak with her son that day.

I reassured her that everything was okay. I also let her know that the wedding was off. I should have kept it to myself, but I was still upset. Then I told her I refused to be with the coward who wanted to blame me for cheating on him. He was the one cheating on me again, instead of breaking up with me and leaving me in peace. I let her know that I was not raised like this, and that this dysfunction had to end. Once I hung up with his mother, I called my best friend back. Before we could laugh and cry together, Daniel was ringing my doorbell.

Still in his clothes from the day before, he came in my place looking pathetic. He was trying to explain his actions, while still accusing me of something that never happened. It was not an apology by any means. I let him know that this wasn't right, and I couldn't marry him. While Daniel's words went in one ear and out the other, he asked me to put my ring back on. He also asked me to set up counseling for every week before the wedding. I let him know that this was unnecessary, because we didn't need to go forward with the wedding at all. I knew that we just needed to go back to being friends, and friends only.

He wasn't listening to anything that I said. He demanded that the wedding go on, and insisted that we were better than all the craziness. I didn't even know what this meant. This was just crazy thinking. Again, we were playing movie roles that he created. It was like nobody was paying attention to reality.

I was expected to be on autopilot, and that is exactly what I did. I was so numb from the emotional rollercoaster, I just played my role. Besides we were so close to wedding, so much money had been spent, maybe he would change.

Questions I should have asked myself:

> What would make you want to walk down the aisle with this man?

> And once again, what would make you marry someone you can't trust?

Advice to my past self:

*Go to counseling independently, and don't marry someone you don't trust.

Tell your parents about what is going on in the relationship. A real support system would never let me suffer with someone like this.

Remember: support systems help you to breathe easy when you feel suffocated. Always keep your support system in the loop when you have to make a hard decision. Crossroads in your life can make or break you.

Weeks flew by. Now I started faking happiness, and we had even deceived our pastor into believing we were happy. I was too embarrassed to come clean about how bad our relationship had become. Everyone was happy that we were getting married—except for me.

It seemed so surreal that we were getting married in a day. All of our family and friends were in town, and we were both joyous as we could be on the outside. On the morning of the wedding rehearsal Daniel phoned me to meet him at the bank. Everyone was rushing to the rehearsal, but I met him at the bank without arguing.

I felt he was up to something again. Low and behold he had a last minute prenup. He was a self-made millionaire and a prenup was his right. The wrong thing was to force it on me last minute. His mother claimed this was no big deal, and that his lawyer had just sent it over late. We were running late to the wedding rehearsal so I didn't read any of it. I signed in all of the marked places so we could get a move on.

Realistically I should have just cancelled the wedding at that moment. It was an appalling way to ask someone to sign a prenup, twenty hours before their wedding. I only signed because I wasn't marrying him for money. I was trying to fix a broken relationship. Clearly, I was in a delusional state.

Since I needed a witness who was on my side, I asked my maid of honor to sign the document. The joke was on them, because my maid of honor was not eighteen at the time. This was something that they did not think all the way through on their end. It was crazy that something like this would even come up. All I did on the way to rehearsal was shake my head at how unreal the last two months had been.

Questions I should have asked myself:

Do you believe your marriage will be less deceitful?

How long are you willing to live like this?

Advice to my past self:

*Just walk away and wash your hands of him. Find a full-time job and finish your degree.

Remember: Leaving a long term relationship is never easy, but you can make it on your own.

That night was rehearsal dinner at a posh spot on the beach. All of the wedding party and our parents were in attendance. We sat and fed each other, as an act, then went our separate ways for our parties. I don't know what revelations Daniel had that night, but I had a big one. My epiphany was I was marrying the wrong man. I wanted a marriage that fell in line with my core values. I needed trust, companionship, honesty, appreciation, and consistency.

I was receiving none of these things, and I was actually marrying the complete opposite. This was a man I had known for a long time, and he was turning into someone

I didn't know at all. His professional accomplishments had gone to his head. It was now impossible for me to be happy with the person I thought was my best friend.

The mistake of carrying on with the wedding was all my fault. I should have never believed that we could be okay. I should have asked my coaching questions out loud. I would have been far away from where I was at in that present moment.

My girls and I were all partying at my favorite club for the night, and enjoying a very low key crowd. In walked Anthony, at the bar, and he wouldn't even look at me. He was the one guy that got away. He was still frustrated that we were not together, and I was getting married. But our break up in the past was my fault so I understood his silence. My heart had fallen into the pit of my stomach. I was still in love with Anthony this whole time. My version of perfect had been in front of me for years, and I messed it up.

We had dated for about a year plus, and even lived together for a little while. Our relationship was fun-loving, and not too serious. We were nineteen and twenty-one at the time, a little young to be so involved. From day one we spent every day together. I was so in love with him I could fall asleep for hours in his lap. I had always felt he was my one true love whenever I was in his presence. I was just too young, and had not seen enough.

Then I jumped into another relationship right after we broke up, and never had time to think. I should have just laid low for a while after Anthony's father passed away, and we took a break. Instead I hopped into another relationship with Daniel four months later. I was swept away by a fake Prince Charming. He was now my nightmare, and future husband.

As I starred at my past I realized my future wasn't so bright.

Questions I should have asked myself:

Would you rather be happy?

Are you willing to face your fear of loneliness to gain happiness?

Advice to my past self:

*Follow your heart. You can feel when something is right or wrong.

Unfortunately, at this point in time being happy wasn't on the menu. I was living outside of my core values, but I could not face the thought of being alone. The point was to be married, and not to be single forever. My falsified version of happiness was clouding my wants and needs.

After my night out with the girls I was so confused. Was there a reason I saw Anthony? Was I doing the right thing? I was more stressed after partying than I was before the rehearsal. Nothing was adding up, but the wedding was only 10 hours away.

At the end of the night I laid in bed with Daniel's younger sister hoping she would help me think things through. I told her how unreal everything seemed, and how it was all so fast. She expressed how she felt the same way, and she didn't know if this was right for us to do. It was so awkward to have heard this from his own sister's mouth.

All of these things let me know that my future husband wasn't true to me, but I was a coward and couldn't call off the wedding. So I slept for maybe 3 hours before waking up for the big wedding day. I woke up very early to start getting my hair and make-up done. Everything was moving so fast around me I couldn't even piece together a full sentence. My thoughts were silent for the first time in a while. I was going to walk down the aisle and become one with the wrong man.

I started to actually question myself silently after my make-up and hair was done.

Are you really okay with marrying this man?

What is another solution to this problem?

The real solution was to walk away right now. Daniel was the wrong man for me. The only problem was I didn't want to talk to anybody about my situation, and say what was going on out loud. The relationship was too crazy for anyone to understand why we were even getting married. Saying he was the wrong man out loud would have stirred the pot. I didn't want to be that person, so I went along with everything.

Then Daniel called me as soon as the bad thoughts entered into my head. He expressed how excited he was to have made it to this day. I was much less enthusiastic. It really was now a movie role, and he deserved an Academy Award. Everything he said sounded so scripted, like he was reading from a romance movie with a happy ending.

Every sweet thing came out of his mouth, down to how perfect I was in his eyes. What he didn't realize was I wanted to hear the exact opposite. I wanted to hear the truth. My ears wanted to hear the fact that our love had ran its course. I wanted to hear we were making a mistake, and that we should stay friends. I knew our love had ran its course and so did Daniel. He just wanted to keep pretending, and I enabled him to do so.

I still had love for my soon to be husband, but I believed he was incapable of truly loving me back. I was not in love with him anymore. This was the man I had known since my high school years. He had been like a great friend I could tell anything. We had so much fun in our past. We had great romance, a lot in common, and all of this had faded over the years.

At one point in time he had given me so much and was so sweet. Now everything he did was for self-gratification. If he did something for me, or anyone, all he did was remind you of how good he was to you. This was no way to live day in and day out.

I wanted to drop the bomb and say that I couldn't marry him, but I also knew how horribly Daniel handled situations that did not go his way. So instead I pretended over the phone like everything was going to be okay. As I sat and joked with my bridesmaids, the time flew by to walk down the aisle in front of 200 plus people.

Chapter Three

Once I stepped into my dress—white with crystals from head to toe—my heart started to flutter. I was so nervous and I had never experienced a feeling like this before. My thoughts now started racing, and I could only think of how this might not work forever. The wedding music started to play and everyone began their walk down the aisle.

This was the definition of insanity! Why was I doing this?

There was no one left in the room except for me and my father, as my wedding song started to play. My father joked with me that I could run and get in my car now to drive away. He started laughing, but what he didn't know was I really felt this way. If my father would have just asked me the question seriously, I would have ran for the hills. Instead I pinched him, smiled, and then we started our walk down the aisle.

---

*Remember: A marriage does not fix things that are wrong in a relationship. It can amplify the problems you have already. You cannot change someone just because you become husband and wife. A marriage should not be used as a band aid or compromise to infidelity.

As I walked down the aisle it was a blur of people, but the only thing I could see was Daniel and the ocean behind him. I don't remember much at all outside of trying to smile. We exchanged personal vows, and he cried like a baby. I, on the other hand, could barely keep my smile going, and there were no tears in sight. It was like I was in my own little world.

After we jumped the broom, we took a fairytale ride in a horse and carriage to the reception hall. Outside we took photos of us, and pictures with our families. After an hour worth of photos we ate dinner, danced, and drank. I barely remember anything except always trying to appear as happy as possible. For me the whole day was like an outer body experience. I don't even remember the wedding night. The next thing I can remember was getting on an airplane to our honeymoon, on a romantic island, to have some fun in the sun.

Once we arrived in another country it hit me that I had married Daniel. I was now so indifferent about the whole situation. Daniel and I tried to enjoy the secluded island, but it was pointless. He was too busy trying to check his cell phone messages, and I was worried about who he needed to hear from. We were on the island for all of three days before we decided to come home.

I knew the decision to come home early from a honeymoon was a really bad sign. We no longer could have fun together longer than a day; everything was just a difficult task. My fears were now becoming the truth. I had been living in denial for so many years, I didn't know how to leave. My relationship was falling apart at the seams, and I was slipping through the cracks.

Two months after the fairytale wedding was over all of the same cheating had begun again. But the real question was, did the cheating ever stop? It seemed like this time around things were worse than before. There were now late night phone calls, text messages from exes, random lunch dates, pictures of him with other women, and now nights of him not coming home. There was no end, and I had helped create this disastrous situation. He was now going out every single day of the week because I was his wife, and he thought I was just there to walk over.

Questions I should have asked myself:

What is making you want to live like this?

What would you rather live like?

What steps can you take to get out of this relationship?

> *Remember: When you let someone disrespect you once it will keep happening. Plus if you act like a doormat people will treat you like one. Nobody deserves to be missed treated, so stand up for yourself.*

These were questions I should have asked myself night after night when I was alone. The lies were coming on a daily basis like an afternoon soap opera. I felt like I was now living in *One Life to Live.* I never knew what lie or story was coming next. I couldn't keep up anymore; everything made me sick to my stomach.

He was even bold enough to be flirting on social media, and lying about it to my face. I guess he forgot that once some things are out there you can't take it back. All of these little things built up within a six-month period. This was crazy, the honeymoon stage wasn't even over, and we were tired of each other. Or at least I was tired of him, and he was just dealing with me.

My tension was high from collecting evidence on Daniel's shortcomings. I started to doubt myself, and wondered if I was going crazy. I thought maybe I was just looking for stuff to pin on a good man. If I left maybe I was giving up 80% good for 20% bad, but this 20% seemed more like 100% sad. I knew searching for things was wrong, but I was over him lying to my face. I needed evidence so that the lies could stop.

I started to find out things that just seemed impossible once we went back east. Was I really married to an individual who would just openly cheat on me? I knew he was not the most faithful, but I never realized things were this bad. All of the rumors from the past that I had ignored were true. He didn't know that people were more than willing to tell me his actions when he wasn't with me. Even some of the women he slept with during our relationship had told acquaintances of mine what was going on in detail. People around town wanted me to know he was cheating.

Then I found out the secret of the century from an acquaintance during a casual conversation. Daniel was hiding a child with another woman. I tried asking Daniel about this child of his, and he would constantly lie and deny it. He claimed he was happy and would never do anything like that to me. I could see his stress, every time I brought up random cheating scenarios. My stress was also building from all of his lies. So I kept searching for the evidence of his hidden child. Every time he left for work I tiptoed around my own home, looking for the truth about our relationship.

As I was washing clothes one morning I found an old phone. This phone would officially send our marriage down the drain. Everything became clearer than it had ever been with Daniel. I was just doing house work, and I was not even looking for anything on him that day. The phone was just right in front of my face, and I figured it was something the universe wanted me to see. The phone was unlocked, which was odd because Daniel had a passcode for everything. I went to the pictures and found more than I bargained for at the time. The phone had very incriminating evidence, with dates and times on it.

I was living my whole life trying to satisfy someone who was already doing that for themselves. I was prepared for the worse as I clicked on every picture. I don't know why I needed confirmation to leave when it was something I should have done a long time ago. There were pictures of him having sex with a number of women just seven months after our marriage. As I kept scrolling, I found more pictures like that, and then a picture of a newborn baby. We were now up to three different women and one child. This was more than enough evidence.

I questioned myself as I sat in our basement:

Was this child his?

Were all of the rumors that my friends told me true?

Did I really want to live like this?

Was my husband leading me in the right direction?

Once I answered my questions I realized I had to leave. My life was in danger. He was my husband, so I didn't use protection with him, and who knows what type of diseases he could potentially pass to me. Sleeping with that many people at once is a statistical health hazard. I had learned in college that his type of behavior was very high risk.

Plus he had a baby! I couldn't believe he had a baby he was denying. At that moment, I went upstairs and started packing my clothes. I didn't want to argue in his territory so I made up a reason to leave our home. I had the perfect excuse because I had outpatient surgery coming up in a week. All of my doctors were still out west so heading back home by the beach was a good lie.

I knew he would lie when I confronted him about the child, and that things could go south so I needed to get away. I was unable to hold on to the fact that I now had proof of his child he lied about. I was so upset with myself for letting things get this far.

One day while he was at work I packed a bunch of stuff in boxes, and sent them to our home out West so he wouldn't know how much I was taking (or ask me why I was taking so much stuff.) My plan was to leave clean and easy, and have him send me the rest of my stuff later. But things never really work out how you want them to in life.

The morning of my early flight Daniel asked if I wanted him to take me to the airport. I told him no, kissing him on the cheek and saying goodbye. I didn't want to make things harder than they should be. I let his cousin take me and my dog to the airport for my flight home. My thoughts were racing, but my mind was set. My husband wasn't leading me in a good direction. He was leading us nowhere fast, and I wanted no part of it.

I started really thinking about what I wanted for my life. I wanted to be happy, and I wanted to be with somebody trustworthy. I knew I could never get that by being in a toxic relationship, so I had to leave.

When I arrived in the sunshine of my hometown, my best friend picked my dog and I up from the airport. With windows down and an ocean breeze, Chelsea and I mocked my horrible marriage by going through Daniel's old phone. We laughed so hard at times we were in tears because the stuff I had on my husband was like a Lifetime movie. Even though we were laughing uncontrollably on the way to my home, I was dying inside.

Every liar and cheater comment, was like stabbing me with a hot knife in my pressure points. I was in a good place though, and realized how bad my marriage was from the outside looking in, finally.

*Remember: The best thing you can do in any bad situation is take a step back. Look at things from an outside perspective. Even write down the advice you would give to someone else. This can help you see things for how they really are. It will even show you the part you are playing in the madness.

When we pulled up to my house I didn't know how to feel. Chelsea left so I could relax by the pool. She let me know we would go hangout a little later that night. Once I got settled in I called my husband's mother so we could go rent a car. My vehicle was still back east so I needed something to drive.

His mother and I had been talking a lot over the last few weeks, and I had discussed with her about my husband being unfaithful. She never really seemed shocked about his actions, but always calmed me down. Though I felt like she had a hand in the child situation, I as able to vent to her.

Her advice was always in Daniel's favor, of course. But she was my person to talk to when it came to details about my marriage, because I was too embarrassed to tell my own mother. After she helped me rent the car, she asked for proof of her son's infidelity. It was my mistake to even let her know that I had proof of his child by another woman. So, I lied to her and said that the proof was at our other home.

After a few moments it finally dawned on me: she knew about his child, and was trying to see if I knew the whole story. All of this was one big cover up, and now I knew why she wanted me to get pregnant so fast. She constantly talked about kids while we were together, and even told me to stop waiting. I knew a child would not make our relationship better, so I never pushed for it. Two and two were finally adding up.

---

*Remember: It is unfair to a child to be a product of trying to make a relationship work. Having children is about love, it is not about being the glue in your relationship.

Questions I should have asked myself:

What was I putting myself through, and for what?

Did I want to continue living a lie?

I needed to get the hell out of dodge, and I was well on my way.

After some days passed without a word from my husband, I knew his mother had told him I knew he was cheating. My only thought was how childish it was for the guilty party to ignore the fact that they were wrong! I should have kept things to myself, but I was desperate to talk to someone. Unfortunately, this action was all a part of the vicious cycle in our dysfunctional relationship.

After I attempted to call Daniel a few times and received no answer, he sent me a ridiculous email. The email was ruthless and tasteless. He tried his usual reverse psychology, but I was done with the games. I responded to the email as nice as possible, and asked him to pick up the phone and call me. I just wanted to talk to him. I wanted to ask him why he married me. I needed some form of clarity, and wanted a casual, honest conversation. Unfortunately, Daniel did not operate that way.

I pondered for days about what to do about my current situation. It was upsetting, but I started actively looking for a divorce lawyer. After having a consultation with the perfect lawyer, he told me to make sure that divorce was the final answer. I now asked myself some really deep questions. This was only the second time I asked myself questions out loud.

Do you really want to divorce Daniel?

Should you try to save your marriage?

Were you willing to sacrifice your values to stay married?

Do you believe this is the marriage for you?

I knew divorce would change my life, so I pondered the decision for days. My emotions were all over the place, and I had no idea what to think. The emotional abuse had definitely taken its toll on me. I had my minor procedure done, and now my head was as clear as it could get. I decided to trust my clear head, go with the flow, and take a step forward. My step forward was to cover-up the tattoo of my husband's name on my body. It was originally done right after the wedding to show my love for him. Now, it was time for it to go away.

After four long hours under the needle, the cover-up was complete. I knew I no longer wanted to be his wife, and it was depressing. But why was I depressed? Wasn't I free to be who I wanted to be now? I needed to get it together, and put myself first. He put me through so much crap, and I was trying to be a good wife to the very end.

The next day I had to call his mom so she could conference call my husband for me. It was unbelievable that I had to call her to get a hold of him. I felt like I was in a fight with a friend in third grade. Daniel was being so immature about the situation.

I remember when he started talking only nasty things came out of his mouth. He wanted my wedding ring back, and for me to take the rental car to his mother. Then he had the nerve to say he was done with me because he was innocent, and I was dumb. What he didn't realize was his old phone was missing and I had proof, with dates, of all his infidelities. I just had to find out who the woman was that had his child.

After the crazy exchange over the phone, I knew what I needed to do. His lashing out gave me the strength I needed to go file for divorce.

This was it: the final frontier and no turning back. There was no more to say and it was so sad. Now I had to tell someone all of the horrible details of my marriage so I could get divorced just a short seven months after our wedding. This was not even close to my dream, or what I wanted for my life.

Chapter Four

When I arrived at my lawyer's office, the next day, I sat down to start filing paperwork for my dissolution of marriage. This was such an intrusive process. I had to give out all of the details about the cheating and violent behavior in our marriage. These were things that I did not discuss with anyone. I was taught that you should not tell anyone about your intimate affairs, and here I was spilling the beans. Unfortunately, I had played the leading role in all of this madness. I had the power to stop it from the very beginning but kept playing along. I told the lawyer every detail about the adultery, violence, the last minute prenuptial agreement, and the child my husband was hiding.

After about two and a half hours of speaking to my lawyer we were all set to go. When I finished talking, the lawyer perked up with a grin on his face. He let me know that everything would be okay, and told me to come back in three days to finalize the paperwork. This was it: no turning back.

On my way to go hangout with Chelsea, I stopped at my home to get some things. When I got there, the locks had been changed. This was interesting because my husband was in another state. I knew right then that his mother was responsible for this action. Our home was none of her business, so I called his father to unlock the door. I could have called the police and changed the locks again, but I was over all of the heartache and pain.

When his father showed up I could only shake my head with nothing to say. By now one of my friends had arrived to help me gather all of my things out of the home. All of these actions were so ridiculous coming from the cheating party.

The questioning started in my head as I gathered things to put in the rental car.

How did you get here?

Why would you let yourself get to this place?

Remember: You always play a part in your own heartache and pain, whether it is passive or active. When you step into consciousness, and learn to be present this is less likely to happen.

I gathered all of my kitchenware and classy wedding presents first. Then my friend and I took all of the photos with me in it, and any card or items I had bought. My intention was not to be childish, but to disappear out of this man's life. He didn't deserve to ever say he was a part of my life ever again.

We took one last sweep of the house before I left the house for good. I knew this was never my home, so it was easy to do. I had come to the lowest point in my life, and I played a huge role in getting there. When I was leaving,

Daniel's father said that he wished things were different, and I gave him a hug with no words to follow. I drove away with nothing to say.

That night I slept at Chelsea's place, and I received a surprising call from Daniel's mother. When I saw her number show up, I was a little angry with her. I didn't know if I should answer or not, so I let it ring a few times before I picked up. She asked me how I was doing, and if everything was okay. This was surprising given that she was the one who changed the locks. I let her know that I was okay, but didn't say where I was staying. I couldn't believe I was having a conversation with her instead of my husband, again. She was definitely helping him, and I felt like she was up to something.

Then she asked if I had filed for divorce, and I told her that it wasn't my plan for now.

She went on to explain how disappointed she was in the whole situation. I was just disappointed in myself for not getting away from this manipulating family sooner. When I finished the conversation with her I was sick to my stomach. I knew she was guiding my husband to divorce me first, and I further knew that she knew about his newborn.

What Daniel didn't realize was that he was being manipulated since he wasn't making his own decisions in a marriage.

Another week passed and I hadn't heard from my husband. Then two weeks later I received hate mail from him, once again putting me and my friends down. He accused me of all the things that he had done, and was trying to justify his own actions. I decided to not give him any leverage over me anymore. As I privately read the email I couldn't believe the wording. I was sleeping on my best friend's floor, and I couldn't even find it in me to cry one tear.

He was being so mean I just couldn't take it. I understood what I wanted out of life, and Daniel was not going to make me sad any longer. As more days went by I felt lonely, and caught between two worlds. My heart was heavy for weeks and I still silently prayed for my husband daily. I just wanted him to be a good husband to me. I was still trying to just be a good wife to him. I didn't really want to be divorced, I just wanted him to love me. But my divorce papers were already signed by a judge, and I was trying to stay strong. Sleeping on a floor should have infuriated me, instead at times I wanted Daniel more.

Questions I should have asked myself:

What will you do if he comes around?

What makes you believe you will be happy going back to him?

How long would it last if you went back?

Are you really willing to keep sacrificing your own happiness?

---

*Remember: You can get stuck in a cycle of dysfunction. Also, you can convince yourself that you are doing the wrong thing by leaving. This is normal, it will be hard to move forward.

It had almost been a full month since I had spoken to my husband. He was now two days away from getting served divorce papers. It was like he had instincts that he was getting served soon, because he called out of the blue. I looked at my caller ID and it was my husband. My first thought was, why is he calling? Then the next thought was, here we go with more cruel language. But he didn't call to badmouth me at all this time around.

When I heard his voice it made my stomach turn. It took me a few moments to even say anything on the line. When he started to talk he had no bass in his voice. He then asked in a pathetic tone why we hadn't spoken. This was mindboggling considering how he was the one who had me locked out of our own home. He was a liar and a cheat, so it was hard to believe anything he said. I was assured he only called to avoid a divorce. My built up anger got the best of me, and I blurted out a bunch of questions.

"How could you just waste so much of my time? Why won't you just tell me the truth? Do you think this is how marriage is supposed to be?"

After my rant I let him know that he was selfish, and that I didn't want to be with him anymore. He listened and had the nerve to say he understood how I was feeling. He just wanted to know if I still cared about him.

Enraged by his tactics to get me to stay, I stopped talking and I let him say his piece. I was curious about his thought process. All he did was apologize over and over. Then the real reason for the phone call came out. Before he got off the phone to head to work, he slickly tried to ask if I had filed for divorce. I was now mad all over again, and asked him if that was the only reason he called his wife. He told me no in so many ways, but I could feel that he was lying. I was tired of all the lies and withholding things myself. So I let him know that I filed for divorce, because we really had nothing left.

I remember his silence was so long that it was scary, and then he started pleading with me. He told me he would call in a little bit and to please answer so we could talk things out. As I hung up the phone I was very confused. I had been sleeping on my friend's floor in a one-bedroom because he locked me out of our house, and now he wanted to talk. I knew he was up to something, but I couldn't prove what it was, so I went to talk to my friend. She told me she did not understand our relationship. At this point, I didn't either.

Chelsea asked me what I was thinking, and I honestly had no idea. I let her know that nothing was surprising to me anymore, and that life was getting crazier by the moment. In my confusion I had every emotion possible. I was angry because I kept trying to be with my husband. I was sad because he was manipulating me. Overall, I was happy because I had left and made the right move towards my future goals. But I was stuck between what I thought was being a good wife, or moving forward as a sane human being.

I knew when Daniel called back more lies would come out of his mouth. Another couple of hours passed and he called again. To see his name pop up on my cell phone screen was very foreign. I answered the phone with the sweetest voice possible to try to be nice to him. I don't remember much, but I do remember him begging, and that was unlike him. I was very short with my answers, and never said more than two words. I didn't even understand why I was talking to him in the first place. I guess I was not fully ready to move on.

Advice to my past self:

*Hang up the phone and stick to the divorce plan. Don't second guess your original instinct.

After hours on the phone we decided to take baby steps. At first I didn't really know what baby steps would be because I was mentally done. But he did a good job of convincing me not to let go of the marriage just yet, and he did it by bringing our religious beliefs into it. After he said a ton of goodbyes, and "I love you" more than once, Daniel got off the phone. I didn't respond because I didn't know what to say.

Questions I should have asked myself were:

Do you believe this is a healthy relationship?

What will it look like to stay married to Daniel?

What makes you feel guilty for being happy without him?

*Remember: You are entitled to be happy in every relationship. You do not have to stay with someone that is making you feel bad about yourself just because you love them. You can love people from afar.

I sat on my friend's couch thinking quietly for hours. I then asked her to weigh in on my options, because I had no idea what to do. She told me it was a choice only I could make. I was so frustrated with myself I went to the gym to run it out at two in the morning. I then had an epiphany on my way back to my friend's house. I thought "Daniel doesn't love you, he just doesn't want to be served divorce papers. He has you sleeping on your friend's floor and could care less." This was all so crazy.

I spent almost the whole night with my eyes wide open. I couldn't believe I was being so stupid. I was the type of person who always encouraged women to be strong and stand up for themselves, and here I was doing the exact opposite. I was considering going back to a man who had betrayed my trust just because he said, "I love you." These were just words his action showed something totally different.

*Remember: Emotional abuse runs deep and is hard to escape. Listen to the little voice in your head, and the advice you would give out to others.

I wanted a successful marriage so much that I was willing to compromise my values. I was only continuing the charade because I cared what others would say. I was subconsciously making the decision to not serve my husband divorce papers. I was keeping myself trapped in unhappiness to make someone else happy. With all of these racing thoughts, I was finally tired enough to fall asleep on my friend's living room floor.

The next morning Daniel called me bright and early to say good morning, and he told me to have a good day. He was still playing some sort of game, but I had no idea what it was at the time. He had timed it and played it so perfectly that it almost seemed sincere. He told me that he was sending me money because he didn't want me to live the way I was living. I then conveniently forgot about the fact that I was living out of a bag because of him. He was so good at saying all of the right things, and I was letting myself get roped back in.

So caught up in a moment of progress toward my goal of a happy marriage, I hoped things would be okay. My mind was playing along, but my inner thoughts were still very weary of his actions. My intuition was telling me something was wrong. It was like a horrible feeling, but I didn't want to say anything. I was letting the same things happen over and over again while expecting a different outcome. This was me going insane.

Why did I let myself get caught in such dysfunction?

I was so invested in being a wife that I looked past all the faults. I loved this man, but I was no longer in love. I even knew that we were wrong for each other, but I was refusing to let go. I knew all the nice gifts and money were the same old tricks. These were all the things he always did after a big fight. One big cycle in a bad marriage.

While another week passed by Daniel and I didn't go a day without talking. Every afternoon we had a conversation about how to mend things. These were unsatisfying, but we went through the motions anyway. Our relationship had become just one problem after another, and I felt the talk was just fluff. We were in need of counseling, but we were still on opposite ends of the country.

I thought that if we started at square one, things would be easier. But like most young couples, we started at square three. The problems for us was always doing things out of order. We didn't have enough knowledge about relationships to have a real marriage in the first place. My parents were divorced, and his slept in separate rooms in the same house. Though we both had seen good marriages from one aspect, some other aspects were not great.

Spending our first Christmas apart was difficult. I had a woman's intuition that something was wrong. I felt like Daniel was being sneaky because he didn't fly me home while we were in our making up period. So I had to spend the holiday without him. Previously, he was rushing me home or was rushing to me, but this wasn't the case. The holidays were a good time for me to be with my family, but I was still very uneasy.

We talked on the phone Christmas morning, and I swore that I heard someone in the background. He was talking very low so that it would sound sincere, but then I thought I heard a distant voice of a woman this time. Conveniently, the phone hung up right after I heard the voice, and then he called right back. He said that he had lost signal in the house, but I knew that he was lying. I was in another state with jewelry, clothes, and money he sent in a Christmas package, all while my husband was spending Christmas with someone else. I couldn't let this feeling ruin the first Christmas I had spent with my family in years, so I put on my game face. I flashed my expensive gifts and smiled so my family would believe everything was okay.

The next day was like any other and we talked for a little bit in the morning. Reluctantly, I decided not to bring up the woman's voice I had heard in the background. There was no winning an argument with someone I thought was a habitual liar. He asked me was I getting excited to see him in the next day or two, and of course I said yes. But the truth is I was still so confused.

All I could really think about this day was why hadn't I served him papers? What could I really do with this relationship? Every time I was around him my self-esteem dropped to a two, but when I was sleeping on my friend's floor I felt like a 10. I knew that this was a problem. But I was still deep down afraid to be alone.

Advice to my past self:

*Your family is there to help you; let them in on how you are feeling.

Remember: Being single is okay. You are never all alone in this world. Fear is your worst enemy when you are trying to progress.

While hanging out at my father's house for a bit my thoughts caught up with reality. Then there was an unexpected knock at my father's door. When I answered, I saw a strange man and my gut got an uneasy feeling.

The feeling was justified because he said, "you have been served." I was now in shock. I thought we had agreed that everything was going to be okay, and that we were not going to serve each other. My thoughts were racing when my dad asked what was going on at the door. I told him that I had been served. The only thing my father could say was, "I told you not to trust that motherfucker. You need to serve him now. Call your lawyer."

As the tension built up in my father's house I stepped outside to call the lawyer's office. My lawyer advised me to come in the next day so they could respond, and also to find out where we could serve Daniel. I couldn't believe I had let this happen. I knew I was being manipulated the whole time, but I was trying to be my version of a" good spouse." There was no more playing nice when he was being evil and self-centered. We no longer had a marriage; this was an act of war. I was now ready to fight dirty.

Chapter Five

After getting off the phone with my lawyer's assistant, I tried to calm down and let my anger go away. I just started reading the paperwork I was served. It was nothing short of comical. I say comical because my husband had filed for abandonment, when I had only been gone a month. And he had filed this after we had started talking again, without telling me. How deceitful could my own husband be?

As I read, I realized that he hadn't filed for divorce, but for legal separation in another state. I didn't want to be separated; if we weren't going to be together, I wanted to be divorced. After I calmed down I took a nice walk to the park. Once I got there I was calm enough to call Daniel and have a conversation. This conversation was more comical than the conversation we had after a month of not talking. I now had removed all emotions, and started just looking at things from an outsider's perspective.

---

*Remember: You have to always take a step back and assess a situation.

When I asked Daniel why I was served with papers, the stuttering began. His explanation was that I told him I had filed for divorce, so his mom told him he should too. He really was following a third party's advice, instead of consulting his wife. I was baffled at the fact that it seemed like I was in a marriage with his mother. These were all the signs to end the marriage. His mother was my significant other, and he was the stand in. My life was a wreck.

As I giggled to myself, I told him now we were getting divorced because I had directed my lawyer to respond to his paperwork. I instructed Daniel to cancel his paperwork if he wanted to work on things. Silence came over him for a moment, then he said he would handle it. But he never said he would cancel it.

Even though I didn't believe a word he said, I agreed to meet him the next day when he returned in town. That night my mind raced with so much anticipation that I couldn't get one ounce of sleep. My thoughts were just all over the place. I read the papers I had been served over 10 times, I looked for marriage counselors, I sat idle at times, and I even managed to shed a few tears. My husband was coming back in town and I didn't trust him.

Advice to my past self:

*Confide in your parents or even your grandparents for advice. You are never too old to seek help when you don't know what to do. Also, don't speak with him anymore, and follow through with the divorce.

Remember: When you feel something isn't right you should not push yourself to do something you don't want to do. I note this more than once because it is an important fact in life. It becomes very important when you are feeling manipulated.

I was trying to not be angry with Daniel, but it was hard to feel any other emotion. He still had too much control over how I operated my life because I allowed it. My anger started to build with myself and with him. I needed to gain my own voice back versus always falling for what he wanted. I thought I had done a good job at this, but I was back at square one with him in control of my life.

My last thought of the night was, "what are you going to do now?" This time I answered one of my hardest questions. I knew I was going to get divorced and be happy no matter how hard it was to do. I just didn't know how to get there. We were not good for one another, and it was hurting who I was as a person.

The sun woke me up the next morning, after I had only closed my eyes for maybe two hours of sleep. I felt instantly sick to my stomach when Daniel called and told me he was on his way to the airport. The sound in his voice was full of excitement, but I did not feel the same way. I was in turmoil over my husband's return, especially after being served legal separation papers.

My thoughts about him were not very nice. I didn't believe a word he said, and I never knew what was going to happen next. Did he really believe misleading me was okay? He had a list of secrets including infidelities. Not to mention, we had not even touched on the subject of him having a child with another woman. I was in limbo, or according to Dante's *Inferno*, the first layer of hell.

To clear my mind of all my negative thoughts I decided to go to the gym for a few hours. After an unsatisfying attempt to clear my head I took a long shower. Then I sat on the bed, in my father's guest room, as I thought about getting dressed to go on a date with Daniel. I didn't want him to know where I was really staying so I took some things to my father's home. His house was closer to Daniel's home he locked me out of, and it was a safe option since he was back in town. Soon my phone rang for our date, and I was nervous. I told him to pick me up at the park around the corner from my father's house. This was because my father didn't want him in his presence.

As I walked to the park my stomach started to feel even more nauseated than before. I knew this sick feeling because I had it before, and nothing good ever happened after its sudden onset. I felt God was guiding me away from Daniel, but I was having trouble divorcing him because I was afraid of what would happen with my life. How crazy was this? I had finally coached myself out of a bad situation, but I was still holding myself hostage. I was wrapped up in my obstacles. Nobody was on the other end holding me accountable to the progress I had made, so I kept taking steps backwards.

My negative self-talk and thoughts were creeping into my reality. Whenever I spoke with my husband, I took a step backwards. My positive thoughts and forward progress were put on hold.

---

*Remember: Coaching yourself is not an easy task. Most people hire a professional to keep them accountable, and moving forward with a realistic plan. It is very easy to backslide without someone's help.

As I sat on the park bench waiting for Daniel to pick me up, everything around me became very quiet, and it gave me more time to think. When I heard his truck driving down the street I believe my heart stopped for a few seconds. He parked the truck so we could talk at the park first. When he hugged me it felt like a stranger touching me. He looked so stressed, with missing patches of hair, and even a sty on his eye. It looked like his mistress wasn't taking great care of him while I was away, and it was sickening that I even felt this way.

While he was silent I was just watching every movement. His phone lighting up from missed texts, even his breathing—every little thing he did at this point made me question the relationship. It had all been a lie from the very beginning, and at this moment I could finally see it. I was not ever going to miss a moment again that God wanted me to see. I was now present and aware of my situation. I just needed some form of closure to officially end our marriage.

*Remember: closure is important for you to move forward in any situation. In all cases it is not always possible, but when you can obtain it make it a priority.

The only word he uttered when he embraced me was, "hi." I returned a somewhat uncompassionate, "hello." Everything was now so awkward between us. He asked me what I had on my mind, and told me I looked great. I told him we needed to get him to the doctor for his sty. I then told him nothing was on my mind, but I didn't know what we should do with one another. He suggested starting at square one, as he had on the phone. He said we should date each other more, and go to counseling. Daniel thought that this was all it would take to repair our relationship. On the other hand, I knew that this was never going to be good enough.

Remember: When you don't have trust in a relationship, the relationship cannot exist.

I let him know my trust levels were at zero, and that I had no idea how to be towards him. As he reassured me that things would be okay, I knew the end was near.

We got off the park bench and went to dinner together at one of our favorite restaurants. This was our first dinner in almost two months, so we tried to share some laughs. This was a big task in itself. Since the college days we had always laughed together, but now there was no more laughter between us. Creating a genuine moment with him was Mission Impossible. Behind every few sentences were awkward silences nestled in thoughts of doubt.

After eating Daniel asked me to the movies. I said no because I was so mentally drained, but I didn't tell him how I felt. I was afraid of his reaction to what I would say. So on the ride back to the park, the only thing we did was listen to music. Though we had spent two months apart, there was nothing left to say. As we arrived back at the park, by my father's house, Daniel asked if we could do another date the next day. This time I said yes. I wanted to see how long the fake sincerity was going to continue.

Unfortunately, Daniel's demeanor was not usually this nice. Before I got out of the car I let him know that we had a counseling session set up in a few days. He seemed very pleased about it, and smiled. I wasn't too enthused about anything so I smiled and said good night. He got out of the car and asked if he could hug his wife. I gave him permission to hug me, but it was so out of place. He held me for a while and said, "I love you, ya know?" But this wasn't true love, so I replied, "I know, this is just hard." We were no longer emotionally husband and wife, but it was so hard to accept. He then drove away slow into the night.

Questions I should have asked myself:

What do you hope to accomplish by seeing your husband again?

What is going to make this time around different?

After my short walk home all I could do was cry. Crying was like my happy release. I cried tears of joy to know that this wasn't the marriage for me. I was just puzzled as to how we had both dragged ourselves into this messed up place.

When I got back to my father's place I had nothing to say. My father asked how it was, and I said it was okay. Things were far from okay, but I knew they were going to be eventually. I just wasn't ready to talk about it yet. My thoughts were all over the place, but my feelings were steady. I didn't sleep that much for the third night in a row.

*Remember: Sometimes it is uncomfortable to talk about your feelings, but in the end it is better letting it out. Try to not bottle up your emotions, it can be very unhealthy.

The next day turned out to be super hectic, and I almost forgot about my rocky marriage. I was out and about doing things to make myself feel good. I even got a surprise call from Daniel's father to let me know my truck had just arrived from the east coast. This was great because I had been without it for almost two months, and driving a rental. But when my phone rang to go on another date with Daniel, reality set in. We were not even living together, he had to come get me. He didn't even know where I was staying. So was he really trying to win me back? Or was he acting like he was trying so he could cover something up?

Questions I should have asked myself:

What outcome are you looking for?

Why are you letting yourself be manipulated?

Still I walked to the park and waited for my date with Daniel. When I got in the car we headed toward a nice restaurant, and a movie this time around. He said sweet things and he used the softest voice possible whenever he spoke to me, but something felt wrong. While we were driving I informed him about our upcoming counseling session.

He seemed enthused that we could get in so soon to see someone. With our first genuine smile toward one another in a long time, we held hands and walked into a restaurant. We discussed many things at dinner, and had fewer awkward moments than the night before. But we were still not functioning as a husband and wife should.

The brief moment of happiness ended when the conversation got serious. I could feel Daniel was hiding something, I started talking about moving back into "our" home. Then like clockwork all of the lies and excuses started. He said he just wanted to wait a while to know that I wouldn't just pick up and leave again. With another person I would say that was a fair response, but he was not that person. He was trying to keep me away from the house, but I didn't know the reason. Once he stopped talking I stared into his eyes, and I could see he was trying to deceive me.

I adjusted to the mood and let him know that I completely understood why he didn't want me home. I was now being just as fake as Daniel, and I felt the mood become very tense. We left dinner and still went to the movie, and I was not a happy camper. He tried to talk to me during previews, but I was not really listening to him. I was bothered throughout the whole movie, and my brain went back into detective mode. It was so sad that I had to investigate to get the truth out of my own husband.

I realized that the trust was broken and irreversible. Deep down in my soul I was so connected to him I knew when he was lying. God had already opened my eyes to the truth, but it was like I needed him to just admit it. How much more was I going to go through? It was like my subconscious had its own agenda, and it wasn't done with Daniel.

After the movie, we enjoyed a snack and a casual conversation. Though my mind was elsewhere, I smiled and nodded. As our night ended I tried to show Daniel that we were making some progress in our relationship. I gave him directions to my father's house so he could walk me to the front door. He got out of the car and open my door for me. He asked if he could kiss me, and I just smiled and said good night. Him kissing me at this point was not acceptable.

Once inside my father's house my mind raced even more.

*Remember when you cannot figure out what is going on in your life you need to slow things down and take a time out.

The next day I knew things were going to be hard. Daniel and I were going to our first counseling session. I was wondering if he was going to tell the truth, or try to lie in therapy. Once we arrived at the counselor's office the part of us we thought we had was gone.

When we started to fill out paperwork he was not being very cooperative. He skipped parts of his questionnaire because he didn't believe the counselor needed to know those things. I answered the questions as honestly as possible, and I even added points of interest. I knew that family background played a huge role in how you view your relationship, so I wrote about mine. His sheet was almost clear, and full of closed answers. This was the wrong attitude to start with in counseling. He was beginning to slowly show his true colors again.

When the counselor came out to get us I was already irritated with the whole situation. She asked why we were both there, and we told her we were trying to save our marriage. Right after that moment it seemed like the lies started flowing out of Daniel's mouth. The first lie was I blamed him for things without any reasoning. When the counselor intervened and asked me why I didn't trust my husband, I told the truth. I told her that he had cheated on me several times, and that he was hiding more secrets. She then turned to my husband and asked was he hiding anything, he then lied and said no. This was his usual response. He always, in my opinion, tried to make me feel like I was wrong, or crazy.

Why were we even here? I knew this was never going to work.

What would make you stay with someone who refused to tell the truth?

What would it take for you to not fear being alone?

Once I reflected on the questions I asked myself at our counseling session, I knew that divorce was the right choice. On the ride home I did have one last question, and I was hoping Daniel would tell the truth.

The question of the year was, "Do you have a baby with someone else?"

He paused and looked in my face and lied. He told me that they were just dumb rumors to make me upset. He was making light of the truth and my feelings about this sensitive situation. I was now really angry. My fire was fueled and I was infuriated at the fact that he thought I did not know the truth. I was now thinking about the perfect time to serve him divorce papers.

Remember: Go with your gut feelings. Your instincts will not lead you in the wrong direction.

Chapter Six

Everybody knows there's no such thing as perfect timing for anything, especially divorce. Two weeks passed, and I still had yet to serve Daniel papers. Plus Film Festival was upon us and only lasted for a week, and I had already waited. I thought waiting another week until after Film Festival was over would not be so bad. I just wanted to have fun with friends, and not worry about divorce. Plus, I had some VIP access to some great parties since Daniel had his hand in some producing.

But to my surprise it would be the weekend that broke everything. This weekend did more than break us as a couple—it shattered any friendship we had left. I was done playing nice, and living up to expectations. They were just my own high expectations I had placed on our relationship that had to stop. My marriage was over and I could not save it alone.

Since we were still not staying in the same home, but seeing each other daily I was helping Daniel with planning things from a far. I usually made all of the plan for his party needs, and this event would be no different. After helping him plan a fun weekend with his friends, I planned my own weekend with my girls. I kept getting funny feelings over the whole weekend, but I was waiting for Monday to file for divorce. In the meantime, I tried to enjoy my weekend, but that did not last long.

Daniel and I had agreed to take the first night of Film Festival weekend and hang with friends. And Daniel pissed me off that very first night because he didn't answer his phone. This was something that we established was never okay when we went to counseling. He thought because we were "doing well" that this was nothing to argue about. He didn't realize that he was not doing well on trying to regain my trust.

Questions I should have asked myself:

What else could you want from someone you let walk over you?

What made you wait on serving divorce papers?

When will you be ready to be divorced?

---

*Remember: Change is a permanent commitment that you have to work on daily, in order for it to last.

I was trying to get through the big weekend, but I could feel something wasn't right. I was more worried about appearances than anything else, but my stomach was still in knots. Daniel finally called me early in the morning after his night out, but I did not answer because I was sick of being the only person in the relationship who cared. I was now trying to consider myself single. I would rather be divorced from Daniel than his doormat.

After four missed calls, from my soon to be ex-husband, I decided to answer the phone. He started off acting like a jerk—not all sappy like had been the last month. Finally, his true colors were showing and we were back to our normal dysfunction. I told him that I was having issues with my knee again and had to go to the hospital. I had an old meniscus injury that would occasionally give me extreme pain, and put me on crutches more than once. Instead of jumping to come get me or meeting me at the hospital, he acted very suspiciously. His only concern was if I was going to make the party he was throwing that night. I knew at this moment he was up to something sneaky. He now didn't care about my health; up to now he'd been hypersensitive.

I went to the hospital and sat for about two hours without any communication from Daniel. I heard more from my girls and Anthony because they knew I was hurt. This did not sit well with me, so I called my soon to be ex-husband and told him I needed to use crutches because I had a partial meniscus tear, again. I was okay to hobble, but the pressure was too much to walk in heels for the party.

Unfortunately, Daniel was more concerned with the party plans and looking good for the cameras. He conveniently told me to just rest at my father's house that night, and didn't even offer to take care of me. This was very strange, since when I was sick or hurt in the past he wanted me within reach. Instead of arguing with Daniel I text him all the information he needed for the night, including transportation. I knew this was it, I didn't argue and he didn't care about my health. We had both given up in our own ways.

*Remember: If you are not important enough for your husband or wife to stop what they are doing when you are hurt, you might want to reevaluate your relationship. Values become extremely important in tough times.

I was now going to be the only person I knew home on the Saturday night of Film Festival weekend. It was okay because I had a big journey ahead with a pending divorce.

Since I had some pain medicine in my system I got a little rest before I was awakened by craziness. Things in my marriage had finally hit the fan, and everyone knew it. My friends were calling because they witnessed Daniel with someone else at the party. This was past embarrassing! I couldn't believe I had let things get this far. We had been together three and a half years, married ten months, and I was not going to stay with him another day. Now even my friends were asking what I was going to do.

I asked details because I was now building a case for my lawyer, and needed information for the discovery part of the divorce. I was on crutches and taking pain pills so I could not go anywhere to confront Daniel so I just called. Of course when I called he didn't answer, and now I was really angry. My anger, this time around, was directed toward myself. I never should have married someone who was a cheater. I set myself up for failure.

Finally, Daniel text me with some lies, and let me know that he was just dropped off by the limo at his house. This was important because I could now get the information about where he went and who was there, since I had made the chauffeur arrangements.

The next morning I called the limo company bright and early. I spoke with the owner and asked for an email of the itinerary with all stops made. I now had the proof of Daniel cheating and picking up another woman. This was it; World War III was about to start. Once I had all the information, I went to Daniel's home to talk. It took me a little bit longer to drive to his home because of my leg, but I was on a mission. Public embarrassment—on top of the disrespect he had shown me and our marriage—was not okay with me. I tried being a good wife long enough, but too much had happened. Daniel was going to do what he wanted no matter how it affected me. I had believed for so long that people were not supposed to get divorced, but this was not healthy for me or my sanity.

> **Remember: You have to take care of yourself. Sometimes the best thing to do is the hardest thing you will ever do.*

When I got to Daniel's house I had to remind myself to remain calm, and to not act out. Once I walked in the house I put down my crutches and slowly limped upstairs. He was playing video games, in the bedroom as a part of his normal routine. I took a seat on the floor because I had a clue what happened in the bed just a few hours ago. He paused and asked how my leg was, and why I was not on my crutches. I told him that I was okay and the crutches were downstairs, but needed him to be straight up about the night before. I told him I knew he was with another woman, and had the proof from the driver. I let him know that lying had to stop because I was over it. I then lied; I told him I would stay no matter what he said because I wanted to know the truth.

I was in no position to fight and be carless, so I just tried the easy approach. He then calmly told me he took his mistress home with him. Then he, finally, told me she was the mother of his child. This was the first time he had admitted it in six months, though I already knew about his child. The information was a great relief to finally hear the truth come out of his mouth. I now knew that my divorce would be for good reason.

*Remember: Somebody who lies to you all the time will tell you things you want to hear versus the truth. Be mindful of the characters you attach yourself to.

Now, my blood was boiling and I couldn't help but say some things out loud I should have held to myself. By the end of the disagreement I just let him know that what he had done was unacceptable and disrespectful. I said I was going home to rest because my leg was starting to hurt. I no longer wanted to look at his face anymore. He never put effort into the relationship, and I was done playing both sides. He thought because he provided money and extravagant gifts that it would all work, but that was far from true.

Questions I asked myself in that moment:

What did I want for my life?

What ultimately would make me happy?

Once I answered both of these questions I realized that Daniel was no longer a part of what I wanted out of life. I started mentally preparing myself for a hard battle, because I knew how mean Daniel would be after he was served divorce papers. Though he was in the wrong, he would believe he could do nasty things. I didn't even turn on the television, when I returned to my father's place, because I was deep in thought all afternoon and night.

The next morning at eight sharp I spoke with my lawyer's paralegal. She advised me to come down and speak with my lawyer in person. When I stepped into my lawyer's conference room, I was fully prepared to lay it all on the line. He was very pleasant and asked me if I was really ready to serve Daniel papers this time. I was now ready and I gave the lawyer two addresses Daniel could be found at most often, and the best times to reach him. I now put my feelings to the side about the situation, and could move forward. Before I was able to leave the lawyer's office I gave him my five-carat wedding ring as a down payment for his services. This was going to go in a lockbox until the divorce was over, and funds were paid. Because my husband was extremely wealthy my lawyer took my case, knowing he would receive cash payment after everything was over. I guess the ring was good for something, because it was not a symbol of a real marriage. It was the symbol of a rich, lonely wife.

Remember: You can make your own money. You do not have to stay unhappy to be attached to someone else's wealth.

These were all events I had never envisioned for my life, but this was now my reality. I was now taking control of the situation rather than letting it control me. As I left the office I felt such a relief, but knew there was more burden to come before the sunshine.

That afternoon Daniel called to see how my leg was, but never asked to see me. He just asked if I was okay with the child out of wedlock situation, and I just hung up the phone. I had no idea that this would be the last conversation we would have as husband and wife.

I was now in the clearest state of mind. Reflecting on everything that had happened up to this point I wanted to beat myself up. I knew I never should have agreed to marry this man after knowing he had been unfaithful in the past. But I also knew that this was just a situation I had to overcome to get to my ultimate purpose, so I embraced it instead of fighting it. I was strong enough to handle the mess I'd put myself in, and I was going to make it out in one piece. I attempted to relax, and spent the rest of that night with my best friend for drinks and a few laughs. I deserved to celebrate my "win" on moving forward.

*Remember: Always treat yourself when you have a "win" in your life. Every "win" is a big deal no matter how big or small.

The next morning my lawyer's office called to inform me that I was on my way to being divorced. My soon-to-be ex-husband was served early that morning. They also informed me how they were handling his filing for legal separation in a different state. They were trying to get it thrown out of court because it was not a valid claim. I was now instructed not to have any more contact with Daniel or his party. Unfortunately, it made for an interesting day full of nasty messages from Daniel. All of the nasty things he said were not going to help his case so I just let it continue.

The phone messages were nasty, but the texts were evil and unforgettable. It was a hard day, but I expected most of these actions. I picked up one phone call at the end of the night from Daniel just to hear what he would say. He was nasty and then said he was coming to get my truck. It was my wedding present so I laughed and hung up. I told my father, and he told me to keep the car in his garage, and he would handle the rest.

Not even an hour passed by before he came by banging on my father's door. He was being so disrespectful it was borderline crazy. My father answered the door and asked him to back off, and gain some respect. They bickered and my father stepped outside and ordered my ex to get off his property before he called the cops. Horrible words were exchanged and then my father came back in and slammed the door.

My dad then advised me to power my phone off, keep the doors locked and to keep it dark in the house. The situation was becoming crazier by the minute. It was a divorce that Daniel caused, and he was being irrational. Plus taking my truck was so ridiculous since he bought it as my wedding present. My father explained that I had to tell my lawyer the very next morning about all of the harassment. Scared and not able to drive to hang out with my friends, I felt frustrated.

When was this nightmare going to end?

The next morning I called the lawyer to tell him about the situation. He asked who the car belonged to, and I told him it was my wedding present. I further informed him that I was the one who went to the dealer to get it, and that my ex's mother used the power of attorney to sign his name.

My lawyer's paralegal told me to go file for a restraining order against Daniel to keep him in check. All of this was so sad, but I knew it was bound to happen at some point. He was so used to everyone around him kissing his ass for money and never telling him when he was wrong. Now I was a target because I was not letting him get his way. While I was at the court house filing for a restraining order, I burst into tears. I had passed my limits on what I could hold inside.

I had to type in the reasons for the restraining order, and I became ashamed of things that happened in the past. It was far from Ike and Tina, but it was not the Brady Bunch either. Given the recent text messages and

Daniel's actions toward my own father, I was so ashamed that I had not ended the marriage earlier.

After putting down every horrible encounter we had, I saw in black and white that our relationship was not what love is at all. This relationship was all about ego. At one point, it was even about my own ego when I didn't end it. Staying in a dysfunctional relationship just to prove things to others was foolish of me. After my tears dried up I called my lawyer's office to update them on the order of protection. They had some good news for me: the case on the East Coast for legal separation had been dropped. They were able to prove that I had not abandoned Daniel, and that he had convinced me to not serve him papers first.

All of the progress for the day was exciting, but the divorce was nowhere close to being over. The paralegal explained that the next step would be discovery, and that it would start that next week. I was feeling good about the day, but on my drive back to my father's house I was pulled over by the police. When the officer got to the car he asked me to step out of the vehicle. I asked why because I was not speeding, and he informed me of the craziest thing. My own husband had reported my wedding present stolen.

Questions I asked myself at the moment:

How low was this man going to go?

What did I ever do for someone to be so vindictive?

I was really shocked by this action, but shouldn't have been at the time. I handed the police officer a copy of my driver's license that still read the same last name as the person who reported the incident. He went to his car and ran the information. When the cop returned he asked what was going on for the car to be reported stolen. I told him that it was a nasty divorce, and could not predict how far Daniel would go. After that I also showed him my copy of the order of protection I had just filed.

The officer let me go, and also assured me that I would not be bothered again. He told me that it was a community property state so I had rights to everything my ex had until our divorce was final. This meant all homes, cars, and whatever I desired to use. I was over it and wanted nothing to do with any of his stuff—at this point I was just numb.

When I got back on the road I had to call my lawyer to tell him about the situation with the car. He said he would put it in discovery and use it in court, but to toughen up because he feared things would get worse.

Worse? Wow! Weren't we at the lowest point when a husband reports his wife's car stolen, and she is driving it?

Once I got home I had to lie down. I had a massive migraine, and I needed just to cry it out. All of the crying was healing my soul. I no longer saw my vulnerability as a weakness because it was making me stronger. I was finally truly upset and could feel it. This was a great thing, because I was not putting myself second anymore. I was no longer a robot, or a doormat. I was conscious and on a better road, despite the madness.

Remember: Try to not bottle things up. It is okay to vent and cry it is a part of life.

I started just questioning all of my actions from day one of our relationship, as a self-reflection tool:

What made me stay with him the first time he cheated?

What made me always hold back how I felt?

What made me not listen to my little voice inside telling me to leave him long ago?

Why would I let someone manipulate my thoughts?

I knew that I would not play victim anymore after reflecting on my answers to the questions. I had always ignored things that were right in front of my face. I played a hefty part in this pot that had boiled over.

My self-pitying moment was over and behind me. I was taking my first action step towards my life goals and happiness. I called the cell phone carrier and changed my phone number. I needed to shut Daniel out of my life all together. Once the number was changed I gave it to family members and four close friends. My circle became very small within a few hours.

Anthony was my closet friend in the world despite our past relationship history. I had been there for him in tough times, and he was now helping me. He was the first person I called when I changed my number. I let him know all of the crazy things that had happened over the last week, and I believe he felt bad about my divorce. The next night Anthony took me out for Valentine's Day. He bought me nice friendly flowers and took me to a low-key dinner between friends. He was an amazing person, and easy on the eyes. Anthony had beautiful teeth, very tall, dark, well-dressed, and worked as an accountant. Our friendship was so strong because we were always there for one another in the toughest times. Plus we never judged one another for our choices in life.

His fun-loving personality helped me smile about my choices, and encouraged me on an amazing level. After the low-key dinner, he dropped me off at my father's home. I knew things were getting better for me because I would catch myself smiling from time to time. I had great support around me, and I was proud of myself.

Chapter Seven

That next week was very taxing. The discovery process was everything but simple. The whole process steamrolled me, and I was not ready for how overwhelming it became at times. Everything I believed my life had been was shattered in the blink of an eye.

The first part of the process was to read our prenuptial agreement in detail, and then for my lawyer to pick apart why it wasn't legal. Besides the fact that I did not have a lawyer present, and it was signed by a witness of non-legal age. The lawyer added the fact that it was one sided and presented to me on my way to our wedding rehearsal. With all of the facts in place the document was considered a null and void.

Next step was for me to sit down with his paralegal the following day to record more evidence of infidelity and cruelty. This day turned out to be even more mind-blowing than the day before. She asked for the phone I had that belonged to Daniel. She also had me go down to our cell phone provider and pull his text messages for six months. I was not sure about doing this, but it was to build a case about his lies and tricking me, so I agreed. Since we were still married I was able to obtain everything she needed quickly.

When the lady at the phone store handed me the thick records my heart started to beat very fast. I could feel the weight of all the lies and deceit without even reading anything. I knew this was the action I should have taken long ago, but was afraid of moving on without Daniel in my life. I knew once I opened the records there was no turning back. I waited awhile before looking at anything because it was going to tell the truth about my whole relationship.

When I returned to my lawyer's office the paralegal took the papers and started highlighting things to help the case. The first timeline she put together was me filing for divorce, and him convincing me not to serve him. The next timeline she put together showed the messages between him and his mother in which they planned to change the locks on our house. Next, she laid out the sweet behavior for about a month, and then the abrupt flip to cruelty and threats. This also included the evidence of him recently trying to take the car away. When the day was over the paralegal gave me my own copy of the records. She told me to read them to reassure myself that I was doing the right thing.

My feelings were all over the place, but I did want to see what this man had been up to. I went to my car and rolled down the windows to read the truth about Daniel. As I read from page to page I could only shake my head at the madness. He was living a very secret life outside of our marriage. He had at least four other women, including the mother of his child. It wasn't like he just had one other woman he was sleeping with—it was ridiculous.

This was who he really was, in black and white. I was finally overjoyed to be getting a divorce, and not putting my health in danger. My husband was engaging in high risk behavior that I was clueless about, and now I could see it all. This was something I should have seen coming from just the cheating I knew about.

Remember: You cannot change someone's habits. When someone shows you who they are believe them.

By the time I looked at the clock I had been sitting in my car outside my lawyer's office for an hour. Once I got myself together I drove back to my father's house. The next two weeks went by really slow because I could not do anything too public. My lawyer wanted me to stay low-key so that my husband's lawyer couldn't dig for things on me.

I had only enough money for the bare necessities; life was moving at turtle speed toward the new me. My lawyer's office called late in the week and gave me so-so news. The first hearing wouldn't be for a month and a half. What was I going to do for six weeks? I could not tip-toe for that long without any type of fun. I would fall into a funk before the hearing. After this news I called my mother to gain some peace of mind, and after that I had a long conversation with a good friend in Florida about my frustrations. He also reassured me that things would work out to my advantage, but it would take time.

After two inspiring conversations that night I just prayed and left it up to the Lord. The next day I started out with making a list of goals and promises for myself. I promised to always love myself first, to always listen to my heart and soul, to not ever put my happiness on the back burner, and to always pursue my goals. My goals were bigger than being the housewife I had been. Some of my goals were: I wanted to finish my degree, start my own company, write a book, help people in need, and empower other women like myself to become successful and happy. After writing out my vision for success I went on a run to complete my daily soothing ritual. Later that afternoon, I drove to the northern part of the city to speak with my mother in person.

Remember: Having a vison board with goals is a very important part of moving forward in life. If you don't know what you want you will tend to go backwards, and repeat what you are comfortable doing.

The long drive was an embarrassing one. I was wishing and praying because I barely had enough gas to make it there. Once I arrived at my mother's place I felt an instant relief from all of my current issues. We talked over tea and sandwiches about most of the things I had been through over the last year. As a concerned parent she asked why I had hidden so much stuff from her. I explained that it wasn't my intention to be secretive, but

I was married, so things were private. I also let her know that there was a lot more, but it was only for me to know. My mother was very considerate and understood my privacy, but was just sadden about the pending divorce.

She asked me if I could leave town for a while so I wouldn't be stuck as a prisoner in my father's home. I told her that I had a free ticket from all the frequent flyer miles I had obtained, but I barely had enough money for a cheeseburger. She understood everything that was happening so she went to her room and came out with a "mommy care package." As I opened bag after bag she kept speaking to me about learning to be good to myself. I told her that being good to myself was the first thing on my new agenda.

Remember: If you don't take good care of yourself, it will be impossible to take good care of anyone else. This is sometimes so hard to do, but it is always necessary.

I opened at least a six-month supply of elegant body wash, body lotion, facial care, and other things a woman needs. The thoughtful gifts put me in tears for more than one reason. She was the best mom in the world, yet I had to keep her in the dark about most of my pain. Also within my care package was an envelope with one thousand dollars in it. She told me this money was for me so I could go south to visit some friends before my divorce hearing. It was enough to feed me for a month, and to give the friend I was going to stay with some money for gas and rent.

Things were working out. I was so tempted to question myself, and to feel guilty for being happy. But I now understood it was my right to be happy, and put myself first. When I got to the gas station around the corner from my mom's house I broke out in tears of joy. I was going to be able to get away from my prison and let loose. Life was crazy, but I was feeling blessed.

I was grateful and smiling because I was going to have enough money to eat. When just four months before this moment I was worried about what expensive car to buy. In hard times I realized what was real and true. Love and sanity mattered; everything else was secondary. I knew material things would come and go, but they didn't make me as a person.

Remember: Do not get caught up in monetary things because they come and go. If money and shiny trinkets are the only things holding the relationship together it will eventually fall apart.

On the drive to my best friend's place, to talk about my trip, I called on my savior down south and made arrangements to fly out the next week. Christopher was doing me a huge favor, and was always easy to vent to. He was an old college friend that I kept in touch with on and off, so escaping to his home would be perfect. The week went by pretty fast as I packed my things and my dog to leave town. It was such a relief to be able to just go anywhere I wanted without the worry of running into Daniel.

The day I got on the plane to take my month-long vacation from divorce, I wrote out all of my thoughts. I was finally focused on making myself a better person. Things were no longer in a grey area—they were black and white.

I had clarity about my divorce, and how it even happened. I was somewhat used to slight dysfunction, so I thought some dysfunction was okay. When I was young, I had witnessed my fair share of arguments and fights between my own parents in the years before they divorced. They were the best and gave me the world, but the bad aspect of their marriage unfortunately stayed with me. Now I totally understood why I made some of the decisions in my own marriage. I watched my parents argue and stay together unhappily, so I naturally thought this was normal.

> *Remember: How you were raised and things that you witness along the way have an effect on you. Take inventory of the things from your past that shape you.*

I stayed in my marriage for so long because I was taught to not quit on a commitment. Nobody had ever told me that it was okay to leave. Even my pastor told me to stay and try in my marriage. My whole situation was nothing I thought it would be, and I was ecstatic to be putting one foot in front of the other again. After writing some "aha" moments down, I realized my plane had landed. I was in a place with beautiful weather and smiling faces. I was finally somewhere far away from my divorce. Once Christopher picked me up from the airport it was time to shake it off and live like a normal person.

I was in a light-hearted mood even though my one checked bag was misplaced on a later flight. There was no need for anger of any kind anymore. I was so happy to be in a new place with old friends.

On my vacation I was so blessed to meet new people who helped me to understand the meaning in everything I was experiencing. I had great conversations with my friend's wife. I told her about some of the craziness I was dealing with. She told me that it was all going to make me stronger someday, and that my story could help others. I was now able to process more things because I didn't have to walk on eggshells. It totally clicked in my head that I was not going through everything in vain. I didn't have to be anybody except myself, and it felt great.

---

*Remember: Always be yourself no matter who you are with or around. Those who matter will always want to see the real you.

I started on a journey of daily meditation, and writing a journal of positive thought. The meditation helped me pull my focus together at times that I lost sight of what was going on. The journal became a habit that I started to pass onto others in my private practice later down the road. It also helped me with daily affirmations, and to stay in positive thought. This made a huge difference in my world because I was able to rid myself of the negative self-talk, and the constant negative thoughts. I filled my mind with thoughts of growth and happiness.

---

*Remember: When you fill your life with positive thoughts it will radiate from the inside out. These things will make you feel good about everything you do, and help get rid of negative self-talk.

When I returned to the airport, a month later, I had a brand-new outlook on life. I was armed with a positive attitude before the court battle begun. Upon landing in my hometown I was just thankful to be safe and sound. I was in a place of total peace and understanding. The divorce was my starting point to a new life.

Upon mastering my feelings I understood that the struggle was to help me grow and learn. This whole process was preparing me for the great things to come in the future. This was just the beginning, not my end. I knew that this struggle was helping me with balancing my life and future. I no longer feared being alone, or needing someone to complete me. I realized I completed myself, and was doing just fine single.

Three days after I arrived back in town I had to go to my lawyer's office to prep for the first day in court. Prep for me was an easy process because I was no longer angry with my husband. I just wanted the divorce to be over. My lawyer and his assistant stressed that I should not get angry, and to just be myself. Now that I had time to reflect I knew who I was again, and anger was not going to be an issue. My lawyer was shocked about how calm I was, but was relieved.

When I left my lawyer's office I went to my best friend's house to move the rest of my belongings from my father's garage to her place. She lived far away from Daniel so it was like being on a permanent vacation. Even though I would be sleeping on her living room floor again I would have more peace of mind. This was a humbling yet fun experience. I didn't have to worry about Daniel finding me, and we could just have fun in her new hidden apartment. We laughed and joked about how Daniel would probably lie in court, and throw little fits. I told her that after my court date I wanted to work for her, doing some little things to help.

The look on her face was funny because I could tell she did not believe that I would work for eight dollars an hour, but I just wanted my own income. It had been way too long since I had my own paychecks, and I didn't want anyone ever to have to feed me again. I was slowly gaining my independence back, and it felt more than amazing. Some people didn't understand why I just didn't stay with Daniel since he was rich, but life was not that simple or shallow. A small income, and my friend's floor, was more comforting than living some rich lie.

The court date came, and the thought of seeing Daniel face to face made me sick to my stomach. There was not enough meditation to soothe the disgust I had for him. I was not sure how court would go so my father came with me. I knew that things would get very interesting and possibly downright dirty, so I needed support. I prayed once we arrived at court for some more mental toughness. I was telling myself happy thoughts and took deep breaths to help control my emotions. I was in knots for the first time in over a month, but I had to testify so the judge could know the truth.

My father and I were escorted by my lawyer and his assistant into the courthouse. We took an elevator up to the courtroom and when we got off the first person I saw was my soon to-be ex, his parents, and his lawyer. Everyone entered the courtroom accept for me and my lawyer. He instructed me to be calm, not get upset, and to just tell the truth. I let him know that I was very nervous, and was feeling weird about testifying. Then I realized this wasn't a fear of mine, and that I was going to be okay. I walked with my lawyer into the small courtroom and once I heard "all rise" my nerves were fine, and my breathing went back to normal. I had nothing to be afraid of, everything was going to be okay.

I was the first to be called to the stand, and it was just like the television shows. My lawyer was the first person to ask me questions, and it went smoothly as planned. Then Daniel's lawyer asked me questions, and it felt like I was being attacked. He was purposely trying to make me upset, and made statements instead of questions. It was a tactic to throw me off my game, but he didn't realize that for me this was not a game. I was telling the truth, and his client was lying to him.

It was funny that while Daniel's lawyer questioned me, he became very upset. At one point I was answering a question and he yelled out, "Not true!" It was so funny to see him get angry, unintentionally showing his character and guilt. The judge told Daniel he could not do what he wanted in his courtroom, and next time he would be thrown out.

Once I was able to step down and take a seat by my lawyer, I felt another layer of stress lift from my shoulders. When Daniel took the stand I silently prayed, and tried my best to block his voice out. He was lying under oath, and trying to stare me down. I only heard the judge scold him about breaking laws on locking me out of the house, and trying to take my car. After that I heard nothing else that was said while he was on the stand. Once Daniel stepped down everyone rose for the judge and then left the courtroom. My father returned to work, and I stayed around to discuss things with my lawyer at the courthouse.

My lawyer assured me that I was in a good position, but to still lay low. He said I could drive wherever I wanted, and told me to just stay positive. He said the judge seemed to not like Daniel too much, so things should work themselves out. I went to my best friend's job right afterward to fill out paperwork because I had to start working so I could make sure I had food to eat. All of my accounts that I shared with Daniel were frozen, for the meantime, so I needed to have some sort of income. After a short day of helping my friend at work, we went and bought an air mattress for me to sleep on. It wasn't much, but it was mine, and nobody could take it from me.

The next day I received an email from my lawyer with another court date, one month away. This was all killing me slowly because I just wanted to be divorced—ASAP. I knew I had to be patient, but it was hard. I started to silently stress and pray less for about a week. Then I got my act back together and kept up with prayer, and doing things daily to keep my life positive. My routine to meditate, write my journal of positive thought, and go on daily runs started all over again. And my life went back into balance with less stress.

Meanwhile, some "frenemies" were updating me on how Daniel was partying on the club scene. They were also telling me about how he went everywhere with the mother of his child. They were trying to make me sad, but I was unbreakable. I was okay with what he did because he was no longer a worry of mine. I realized that some of these friends were fake so I started cutting people off one by one. For now my circle was my best friend, my parents, and Anthony. These were the only people who understood how painful the process of divorce was to me. They were also the only people I trusted to know where I was laying my head at night.

---

*Remember: When you go through tough times you will find out who really has your back. It is okay to let people go, but it can be hard.

The next month went by fairly quickly as the second court date approached. But, before the court date I received a personal call from my lawyer. The phone call from him personally was rare. He explained that there did not have to be another court date, which was a relief. He told me Daniel's lawyer wanted to settle before going in front of the judge again. My lawyer said that this was great news because I could get the divorce over with soon, and start my new life. Then my lawyer asked me what I wanted. This part was very hard for me. I didn't know how to ask for anything from Daniel.

The questions I asked myself were:

Did I really deserve to ask for anything?

Was it my right to any money, homes, or cars?

I was quiet for a while because I was trying to reflect on the past, present, and future. I decided that my ex could have all of the stuff, even my customized truck. I didn't want to have anything that he had paid for in my life anymore. I wanted to make the divorce as painless as possible. I gave my lawyer a nice round number of what compensation I deserved, and he said that the number was more than fair. He asked did I want more, but I was not interested. I didn't want anything else from Daniel.

I spent the whole day glued to my computer emailing back and forth with my lawyer. The counteroffer came with more money, but required me to give up my dog and my 5-carat wedding ring. This was an insult because my dog was the best thing in my life, and the ring was made for me. Daniel was still trying to be vindictive, even though I passed on fighting for a house, or my car. My response to the counteroffer was no because he had no right to try to take my happiness. Daniel knew my dog was my stress relief and a big part of my happiness, so he was trying to push buttons. Because of the silly counteroffer the day finished without an agreement, but I could now smell my freedom.

I went to work later on with a grin from ear to ear. I knew the Lord was working his magic in my life, and nobody could stop it. My plan of action was coming true. The first goal on the short-term list was to get divorced and I was close. The next short term goal was to just have a blast and make my own money. I was no longer stuck like I had been for years, I was happily moving on one foot in front of the other.

The night passed quietly, and the morning came peacefully. I awoke to the most joyous email in my life: we had an agreement with Daniel. The next step was to go sign the papers, but it would take a few days for the lawyers to draw everything up.

Questions I asked myself:

Would I be single forever?

Would the next guy understand my past situation?

Was I really going to be okay being on my own?

---

*Remember: Ask yourself questions about your fears, so you can face the fears head on. You will see that your fears are not that bad.

The next week, when I was going to sign my divorce papers, it dawned on me that it was really over, and that I would eventually meet someone nice. Once I got to my lawyer's office I was excited to initial and sign on all of the tabs for a dissolution of marriage. We arranged a time for me to return the car, and for my ex to mail all of my things from the other home to my lawyer's office. This was all a part of our sealed agreement. Before leaving the lawyer's office, he returned my wedding ring to me out of the safe deposit box. By now it had no sentimental value to me, but it was worth a pretty penny. I had sold all of my other jewelry to a private dealer, and this piece of jewelry was next. I intended to rid myself of all things that reminded me of Daniel, and this included shoes, purses, and even clothes.

I now had to wait 60 days for the state to send me a sealed version of the divorce papers before it was fully legal, but I was free and single. Two months passed by fast and I pick the sealed papers up from my lawyer's office. When I arrived at the office I saw another associate lawyer as I was walking into the building. He stopped me to talk, and to give some words of wisdom. He encouraged me to not let the divorce make me angry or bitter. He said to look at everything like a teaching tool, because I had plenty of life ahead. The last piece of advice was to stay open to love and marriage. Fortunately, I was open to being happy in all aspects of my life.

When I picked up my enclosed envelope of divorce papers, I also picked up my settlement check. Everything I had been through was priceless, but to live comfortably again was a great feeling. I didn't even cash the checks the first day; I only read my divorce papers word for word. It was in black and white with a state seal on it. I was free. Once I got back to my friend's place I sat on my air mattress, and wrote a poem to release all of my thoughts:

The End

Life is what you make it

That is what I am told.

People don't understand

How another can touch your soul.

Take you for granite, and then hurt you more.

More than you intended for them to have control.

It's my life, not yours!

Still you have touched my soul.

My life, but your wife!

What is this mess I am in?

It is my self-esteem,

Still you have crushed it.

It is my dream,

And still you have altered it.

Give it back. Give it back.

I am not yours,

We are not one.

A wife running like a runaway slave

Drops to her knees and asked, "Why?"

This is my life, this is my life

But still I am his wife.

To exit a marriage in a manner that is becoming of a woman

Is the hardest road to walk.

There, over there,

Is the light I searched for

At the end of the tunnel.

For that man disappointed me as all people do.

I made it out with only an ounce of faith, but

My life was now brand new.

Now I understand how another can touch your soul,

Disappoint you and hurt you more..

You can lose yourself and fall apart,

But don't be afraid to build yourself back up.

I am once again whole and new

Good self-esteem and no mess from you.

I am everything more, and nothing less.

My life and not his wife!

A part of me felt some sadness about the divorce on some days. This sadness came from built-up frustration, and didn't last longer than six months. I had always imagined the process being more painful, and that is why I feared being single. I thought being divorced was like broken glass, but I was wrong. Divorce was the easy part. The hard part was finding myself, and not letting anyone alter the process. At this point I was slowly transforming into a better version of myself.

My last name was changed back, and now I was taking a step towards having fun and being purely happy. I moved out of town so I wouldn't have to bump into

Daniel anymore. I chose the wonderful city of Las Vegas because it was known for its fun. My time there was spent being happy, and making a great living on my own. It was a great place to transition from my divorce to being confident and single. I was now no longer down playing any of my desires in life, and I was okay with being alone. I was really living life for me and nobody else.

The forward progress I made with my own happiness helped me establish my identity again. I was no longer just an extension of someone else, I was important too. I reworked all of my struggles to see the lessons I needed to learn in life. I knew now that if something felt wrong, I should go with my first instinct. These lessons and going with my feelings, eventually, saved me from a lot of heartache and headaches. Now I understood that you create your own frustration, so you must make better choices. I could see life so clearly, and was happy it happened in the way that it did.

The best lesson I learned from my relationship was to achieve balance in my life. I also learned to live my own life not someone else's life. Losing my own identity was the worst thing that I ever let happen, while in my relationship.

It was amazing how I started to achieve balance through aligning my mind, body, and spirit. Being in balance helped me find my purpose, and my version of success. Once I balanced my mind I learned to think positive on the daily basis. It was essential to keep negativity away from my growth process. The process to about three months, but once positivity sunk in, my life was better. I only kept people around who had positive input about how I was creating myself. I than realized that toxic people were holding me back.

*Remember: Positive thinking is essential. If you have people in your life who are discouraging you, you might want to reevaluate their impact on your life.

Aligning my spirit was trickier, and it is still a major part of my daily upkeep. I pray and meditate daily to help relieve stress. This process also brings me to a place of gratitude, which I need to remain positive, and grateful for my story. As I aligned my spirit I also had to learn to control my emotions, and understand other individuals' perspective. This was the key to not getting upset anymore. It was also the key for me to truly accept others for who they are, and not who I want them to be.

*Remember: Perspective is everything, you can learn positive things from every situation.

The last part of my balancing process to transform my life was to align my body. For a while during my relationship and divorce, my hair was falling out, face was full of acne, and I was always tired. The stress level I was dealing with was not healthy to my body. I was occasionally not eating, and when I ate, it was fast food.

I learned that going on a run occasionally, or to the gym was not good enough. I started eating a very clean diet daily, and exercising four to five days a week. Caring for my body inside out really helped reduce stress, and even provided more energy for important things in life.

Remember: Taking care of your body is important for your well-being, and important when making a life changing transformation.

I was transforming into the best me. I was able to reestablish the secure version of myself, and move onto a loving relationship. This was a relief compared to the anxious-insecure mess I had been over the last couple of years. Finally, I was happy with myself and accomplishing all of my goals. I chose happiness and even got married to Anthony. He was indeed always the one for me. This taught me to relax, and to let life flow because nothing will happen before its time.

Remember: If you don't know why you are in your relationship, it is time for you to start reflecting on your intentions. Some of us get married out of wants and needs versus true love. But you have to truly love yourself first, to truly love someone else.

Printed in the United States
By Bookmasters